THE LURE OF THE LANCASHIRE WITCHES

The Lure of the Lancashire Witches

Jennie Lee Cobban

Published by Palatine Books,
an imprint of Carnegie Publishing Ltd
Carnegie House,
Chatsworth Road,
Lancaster, LA1 4SL
www.carnegiepublishing.com

ISBN 978-1-874181-79-8

Designed and typeset by Carnegie Book Production

Printed and bound in the UK by Short Run Press, Exeter

Contents

Acknowledgements   vii

1   The Weird Sisterhood   1

2   Dolls of Clay, Fairies and Familiar Spirits   25

3   Witchwood, Witchstones and Old Shoes   49

4   White Witches, Written Charms and Witch Bottles   73

5   King Charles I and the Supernatural Roadshow   95

6   The Charm of the Lancashire Witches   117

7   The Wonderful Witches of Lancashire   133

Endnotes   149

Bibliography   165

Index   171

Acknowledgements

I would like to offer my heartfelt thanks to Community Heritage Manager Sue Holden, and all the other staff at Clitheroe Library who have gone out of their way to help with this project. Thanks are also due to the Rochdale library staff at Touchstones, and at Rawtenstall and Burnley. I would like to thank the following for their invaluable assistance: Laurence Inwood of BBC Manchester, Mike Townend of Towneley Hall, Heather Millard, Simon Forster, Dorothy and David Winstanley, Ruth Nutter, Rebecca Shawcross, George Wolfenden, Derek Tree, Bryan Sitch, Paul Jackson of The Dalesman, Molly Haines, Alice Nutter, Carol Clemson of Bull Hole Farm, Harvard Law Library, Annabel Spenceley, Debbie Wadsworth, Mrs Kay, Mr Berry, and Maureen Stopforth of Witches Galore. Many thanks also to Peter Ogilvie of Salford Museum and Art Gallery, Rachel Jackson of Clitheroe Castle Museum, Miles Whittaker, Chris Collyer, Colin Carr, David Knight of Stonyhurst College, Stuart Mason and Greenwich Heritage Centre and Moorhouse's brewery. And cheers, finally, to my sons Daniel and Edward who read the proofs and who were dragged around several gloomy graveyards, became stuck in cattle grids on remote Pendle farms and provided moral support on research trips which at times resembled stepping into a particularly creepy horror film.

Jennie Lee Cobban
2011

This book is dedicated to:

Ralph Merrifield
1913–1995

&

The Lancashire Witches
R.I.P.

CHAPTER ONE

The Weird Sisterhood

Imp and witch, to the Malkin gate,
In all strange shapes, assemble!
Gather, till with the fiendish weight
The old walls shriek and tremble!
Snake from muddy pit, toad from tomb,
Cat from the cottage ember;
Hurrah for the hell-broth, banquet, broom,
Blue fog, and black November.[1]

n the beautiful and bleak Forest of Pendle in 1612, two elderly and infirm ladies had been snapping at each other's throats for several years. No ordinary old ladies, these. Both lived in the shadow of the bewitched and bewitching Pendle Hill and vied with each other for the title of most powerful witch in Lancashire, for in those days Pendle Forest grew witches rather than trees.

In the red corner stood Elizabeth Southern – almost blind and in her eighties, and known as Mother Demdike.[2] Supporting the old lady was her extended family comprising her widowed daughter Elizabeth Device (known as Squinting Lizzie), along with Device's children – Alizon, James and young Jennet.

Demdike and her brood lived at Malkin Tower, the location of which has long puzzled historians, but which in all probability lay in the vicinity of Newchurch-in-Pendle.[3] Their legendary home may have taken the form of a cottage attached to an old peel tower designed to provide protection against Scottish raids in the fourteenth century.[4] The women of the family scraped a living by begging such unappetising commodities as sour milk,[5] along with occasional day-work, while James was described as a labourer.[6]

Demdike was known as a woman who cured cattle, and had no doubt passed on certain talents to her younger relatives. White-witching could be quite a profitable sideline for those on the breadline, and few would dare refuse charity to

a wise-woman capable of harming as well as healing. Demdike certainly seemed to be happy to do both. The whole family must also have been eligible for poor relief, and it is a pity that the churchwardens' accounts recording the witches' names are no longer extant.

Facing Mother Demdike and her family in the blue corner stood another wise-woman, Anne Whittle (or Chadwick), known as Mother Chattox – also in her eighties – together with her two daughters – Bessie and the widowed Anne Redfearn. Chattox and her daughters lived on land belonging to the Nutter family of Greenhead. The Chattox house was probably located in West Close, but again, the exact whereabouts of their home has been forgotten. Richard Catlow suggests that they may have lived near Pendle Hall Farm at the bottom of Ightenhill Lane, as a ruined building there was traditionally known as 'the witches' cottage'.[7]

That the two elderly wise-women had once been on friendly terms seems beyond doubt, as they used to share charms with each other. Relations appear to have soured over the years to the extent that Demdike's son-in-law, John Device, actually paid Chattox a measure of meal every year to leave his family alone, suggesting that he considered Chattox a more powerful witch than his mother-in-law. In 1601, however, John Device died and the payment of meal was not made to Chattox. Furthermore, on his deathbed Device accused Chattox of bewitching him to death. Deathbed accusations of witchcraft were very common and possibly due to the dying person running a high temperature due to infection, which can often lead to hallucinations. My father, recently in a similar situation, claimed that a lump on his arm had been caused by 'that witch at Waddow'. He also insisted that the nurses in his ward convened at dawn to have a riotous witches' meeting. This was from a man who had not the slightest interest in the subject of witchcraft. In the seventeenth century such unfortunate delusions might have resulted in fatal consequences for some hapless person.

According to Alizon Device, Chattox swiftly retaliated to the loss of her tribute and accusations of witchcraft by sending someone to break into the Device cottage (Alizon calls it their 'firehouse', the everyday term for a dwelling), to steal goods worth 20 shillings.[8] This represented a substantial loss, probably wiping out the family's finances, such as they were. Relations between the two families took a further nosedive when a daughter of Chattox was seen parading round wearing some of the stolen items.

Over the next few years, relations between the two witch families must have resembled a powder keg requiring only a tiny spark to ignite a massive explosion of ill-feeling. That spark was provided by Alizon Device, who on Wednesday 18th March 1612 lamed a pedlar called John Law. This act eventually sealed her fate and led to nine men and women swinging on the gallows on Lancaster Moor four months later.

It was probably quite early in the morning on that fateful Wednesday when Alizon met the pedlar on a road called Colne Field. She was on her way into Trawden Forest on a begging expedition while he was more than likely on his way to Colne to sell his wares, it being the town's market day. Pedlars were not highly thought of in society; their status was considered no better than vagrants. Alizon and the pedlar were probably on about equal terms as far as their social status was concerned.

Their encounter has been described many times – how Alizon asked him for some pins and the pedlar refused to undo his pack, leading to some heated words. Whereupon, according to Alizon's confession, she snapped an order to her familiar spirit, a black dog, 'Lame him!' The pedlar had not gone a hundred yards before he was struck down with all the symptoms of what we would today describe as a stroke. Law was carried into a nearby alehouse in Colne (possibly The Dog, demolished in 1790) into which Alizon followed him. Awestruck at her own power, and presumably feeling very apprehensive of the consequences, the young woman then resumed her journey to Trawden. She was right to be anxious, for a few days later the pedlar's son, a clothier called Abraham Law, stormed in from Halifax and furiously insisted that action be taken against Alizon for *maleficia*. And so it all began.

The magistrate before whom Alizon was dragged was the 30-year-old Roger Nowell of Read Hall, an experienced administrator who had already served as High Sheriff of Lancashire in 1610. His fellow Justice was Nicholas Bannister,

Read Hall, the home of J.P. Roger Nowell, where several of the witches were interrogated

aged 70, who lived in the medieval moated hall at Altham. These men had probably been aware of the antics of the two witch families for years. However, faced with a man from outside the area who was baying for blood, the two magistrates seized their opportunity and took the action which would result in the local wise-women being re-cast as malevolent witches. It only took one tentative step into the dark side to change people's perceptions, and Alizon had positively bounded there.

As enquiries proceeded, Alizon dragged her grandmother into the mess, and it seemed inevitable that Chattox and her family would also be implicated by the Device family. Evidence from various sources suggests that suspected witches were generally searched for witch marks and watched by guards in their own homes while investigations proceeded.[9] In a later incident in 1620, about which we have no further information, the household accounts of the Shuttleworths of Gawthorpe Hall record that a payment of *xxijd* was made to the Constable of Padiham 'towards the watching of the *supposed wiches*'.[10]

Having questioned the women formally at Read Hall and an unidentified house in Fence,[11] within a few days Nowell and Bannister had amassed enough evidence against Alizon, Demdike, Chattox and Anne Redfearn to send them to Lancaster. Nowell would have had no fear of being bewitched by the accused during his enquiry, as King James made it known that when she was apprehended by a magistrate, the Devil revoked the witch's power to harm.[12]

Once witchcraft had been alleged, nobody seemed to be able to shut up about it. Accusations flew between the two families like swarms of angry wasps. Demdike had seen Chattox and Anne Redfearn making voodoo dolls of their victims, James Device had heard that Chattox had taken teeth from a skull in Newchurch graveyard and so on and so forth. More disturbingly, Demdike's family seemed set on self-destruct, as they blithely accused each other of possessing familiar spirits and performing malevolent magical acts. We can only assume that they were told mendaciously that if they came clean, everything would be fine. None had the benefit of education, or enough legal knowledge to realise that they were confessing to, and accusing others of, crimes carrying a capital sentence. Demdike, Alizon Device, Chattox and Anne Redfearn were duly packed off to the gaol in Lancaster Castle on 2nd April to await their trial at the assizes in August.

Having delivered the witches into the hands of the formidable Thomas Covell, the gaoler of Lancaster Castle, Roger Nowell probably heaved a sigh of relief and thought that that was the end of the matter. However, within a week he was hearing reports of a 'great Assemblie of all the most dangerous, wicked and damnable Witches in the County farre and neere'. Events were about to take an even more dramatic and bizarre turn.

The Meeting at Malkin Tower

The celebrated assembly of the witches at Malkin Tower took place on Good Friday, 10th April. As witch assemblies go, it wasn't terribly exciting. No horned devil presided over a midnight feast while demanding obscene anal kisses from his evil slaves, and there was a distinct lack of naked dancing and singing around cauldrons.[13] The Lancashire witches' assembly took place at midday in broad daylight, and all the so-called witches actually did was make a nice meal of a lamb that James Device had stolen from John Robinson of Barley.[14] Present at the feast was Jennet Preston of Gisburn, who had within the week been found not guilty of witchcraft at the York Assizes.[15] Katherine Hewitt and Alice Gray (who were presumably family friends) also attended. Neighbours such as mother and son Jane and John Bulcock of Moss End also turned up, along with family members including Christopher Holgate (Demdike's son) and lastly Alice Nutter of Rough Lee, a widow of about seventy who was probably a friend of Demdike.

Elizabeth Device's aim in calling everyone together for a crisis meeting may have been to obtain advice about how best to help Demdike and Alizon when they were tried at Lancaster in the coming August. She might also have sought advice about how those still at liberty should conduct themselves to avoid any further trouble (having a big secret meeting was certainly not the way to go). Jennet Preston, having just been through it all on 2nd April in York, would certainly have been able to advise on how the trial procedure worked, having survived the experience unscathed on that occasion.

However, according to the information given to Roger Nowell by child-witness Jennet Device, the meeting had been called to discuss far more sinister objectives. These were to christen Alizon Device's familiar spirit, kill Thomas Covell (the gaoler of Lancaster Castle), blow up the castle, and release the prisoners. Before we laugh, it should be noted that Lancaster was by no means a completely secure fortress. In Lancaster town and further afield, offers of reward were often seen for the capture of escaped prisoners, such as John Thules, a Catholic priest who escaped from Lancaster Castle in 1616.[16]

It is possible that Jennet, being but a child, had got hold of the wrong end of the stick, taking throw-away comments seriously. When discussing how to proceed and how best to help those imprisoned in the castle, someone might have passionately shouted something like 'Let's blow the bloody place up and kill Covell!' And if we consider the possibility that the suspected witches present at the meeting were not quite the weak-minded peasants portrayed by 'court reporter' Thomas Potts, then Nowell might even have considered an attack on the castle

King James I sitting in judgement on the Witches of North Berwick (Woodcut, Newes from Scotland, 1591)

to be a potentially genuine threat. We should remember that Guy Fawkes and the Roman Catholic gunpowder plot of 1605 were still very fresh in the minds of the Protestant elite who seemed equally paranoid about the threat posed by Catholics and witches.

The alleged intention to christen the black dog – Alizon's spirit – is more problematic. According to most statements given in witchcraft examinations, witches did not give names to their familiar spirits. The familiar told the witch what its name was, not vice versa.[17] A misunderstanding may have arisen as a result of an incident reported in an early tract on witchcraft called *'Newes from Scotland'*. This described how King James I was victimised by a group of Scottish sorceresses known as the North Berwick witches. They supposedly formed a coven 200 strong and performed a ceremony in which a cat was christened.[18] The animal was then butchered and thrown into the sea in a spell designed to create a storm. This was intended to sink King James' ship as he was sailing back from Denmark with his fiancée. If Lancashire J.P. Roger Nowell had read this tract (which he probably had), he may have asked a leading question involving christening animals to work malevolent magic. This question may have been completely misunderstood by the accused witches, resulting in Nowell unwittingly obtaining evidence of the unique and non-existent Lancashire practice of christening familiar spirits. Bizarrely, this information would then appear in future legal guidelines as one of the things witches were known to do at their meetings!

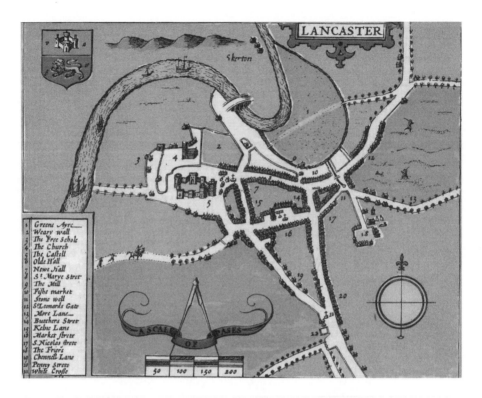

Plan of Lancaster, c. 1610
(Reproduced by kind permission of the Historic Society of Lancashire and Cheshire)

The Dungeons, Thomas Covell and the Death of Demdike

The meeting at Malkin Tower provided enough evidence to send the rest of the Device family to Lancaster to join Demdike and Alizon, along with many others who had attended the gathering. Wisely, many fled before they could be placed in custody. This included Christopher Holgate – Demdike's son – who was really rather skilled at evading arrest.[19] He managed it a second time twenty-two years later when he was accused of attending another witch meeting! The next batch of accused witches left Pendle and followed a route through the Trough of Bowland to reach Lancaster. After several hours of bumping along the rough track in a cart (the able-bodied possibly trudging on foot), the party finally approached Lancaster by way of the moor on the eastern side of the town.

As they were transported along the rough track of Moor Lane, one of the first things to catch their gaze was the melancholy sight of the triangular gallows.

In 1612, the
condemned witches
travelled to Lancaster
on this road through
the Trough of
Bowland

Lancaster Castle

The dungeon in the
Well Tower where,
according to tradition,
the witches spent
their last days. Notice
the ring in the floor
mentioned by the
writer Cross Fleury
(Photo Courtesy of
Mick Ross)

Shortly afterwards, a few scattered timber houses with thatched roofs appeared alongside the road. Having passed through the little square called Stonewell, they probably approached the castle by way of Market Street rather than taking Church Road, as the latter would have taken them past Old Hall[20] and through a rather well-to-do area boasting some new stone houses. (The last thing the richer citizens of Lancaster would have wanted to see from the window was cartloads of bedraggled witches being driven past their front doors, although it is always possible that they would find such a spectacle entertaining.)

Finally Elizabeth, James and the others were faced with the imposing gateway to Lancaster Castle, possibly obscured slightly at that time by cottages which had been built in what used to be the moat. These were demolished in 1874 to improve the view. We can imagine the men and women gulping in apprehension as they noticed decomposing quartered remains of executed criminals hanging from the walls, and perhaps a rotting head or two rammed onto spikes mounted among the battlements.

Once they were inside and the dread gates had been slammed behind them, we cannot say exactly where the latest batch of Lancashire witches was taken. They may have joined Demdike and the other three prisoners in the Dungeon Tower (known as one of the most loathsome prisons in the country), where George Fox, founder of the Society of Friends, is thought to have been imprisoned in 1664. Fox left a vivid description of his privations, saying that the smoke was so thick he could barely see a lighted candle, and it rained in on his bed so that his shirt was constantly wet through.[21] The conditions that the witches were kept in were probably far more extreme.

Traditionally, their place of immurement was the Well Tower, known today as the Witches' Tower. Unlike the Dungeon Tower, the Well Tower still stands but is unfortunately at present inaccessible to the general public. This awful prison was visited and described by writer Cross Fleury who visited it in 1891:

> The dungeon is a dungeon indeed – a veritable inferno of gloom, that sort almost capable of being cut with a knife. There is not a ray of light. Death in her angrier form has reigned here. Many feet below ground you descend, and note the iron rings to which the sufferers were fastened – fastened to the floor; note also the two heavy iron doors with their double locks. On the right, as we ascend the steps of the dungeon, we see a deep opening, and ascertain that it leads down to a well …[22]

It all proved too much for poor Demdike, who died before she could be brought to trial. Gaol fever and plague spread easily in filthy prison conditions, but it is not known what precisely killed the old lady. It might be argued that the gaoler, Thomas Covell, was technically guilty of felony as he had failed to keep the old lady alive for her trial. As she had been found guilty of no crime, presumably she was granted a funeral in Lancaster along with a Christian burial, and may even be buried somewhere in the grounds of the adjoining Priory. Her son Christopher Holgate was, as far as we know, the only family she had left. He was on the run and in no position to collect Demdike's body and return it to Pendle.

Thomas Covell, the Judges and the Trials

As well as being technically accountable for the death of one of the witches, it might reasonably be alleged that Thomas Covell had other things to answer for. He cannot have regarded with any sympathy or goodwill those prisoners accused not only of witchcraft, but of planning his own demise. All those present at the Malkin Tower meeting may well have received violent treatment at the hands of their gaoler. Vicious maltreatment and violent irregularities were traditionally

POTTS AFTER BEING THROWN FROM HIS HORSE.   P. 224

The Londoner Thomas Potts
being hassled by Lancashire locals
(Illustration by sir John Gilbert, 1854)

associated with this office.[23] While torture was officially illegal in England, there is every reason to think James Device in particular received some very rough handling. We are told by Thomas Potts that Covell had taken 'very great paines' with James during his imprisonment 'to discover his practizes, and such other Witches as he knew to bee dangerous'.

When we are subsequently told by Potts that James (who was, we should remember, a labourer) was unable to stand or speak at his trial, then it seems we must certainly consider the possibility of torture by Covell and his minions.[24] At the very least, James may have received the same treatment as St Edmund Arrowsmith, who in 1628 was placed in heavy chains and thrust into a 'Little Ease' cell similar to that in the Tower of London. This was pitch black and so small it was impossible to either lie down or stand up, forcing the victim to crouch in a backbreaking position. Its present location is unknown.

Contemporary opinions regarding the character of the castle's gaoler – who held that position for 48 years – were very mixed. While the puritan Henry Burton described Covell in 1637 as 'a beastly man', John Taylor, the 'water poet', described him in verse in 1618 as 'kind Mr Covell'.[25] He was certainly much more than just a gaoler. Mayor of Lancaster six times, coroner, Justice of the Peace and at one time an alehouse keeper, Thomas Covell was a very powerful man indeed, and must have terrified the likes of James Device out of his wits.[26]

As August approached, Covell began to make preparations for the arrival of the two judges who would try the accused witches at the Assize. He was responsible, at his own cost, for the provision of lodgings (at this time located in the castle) for the judges and their servants and for making sure plentiful food was provided for them at the Sheriff's table.[27] The Sheriff himself provided wine, sugar and venison for the judges and his own staff.[28] Sheriffs were appointed for one year and in 1612 the position was held by Sir Cuthbert Halsall, known later as 'bad Sir Cuthbert' when he ended up in prison for debt in 1631. Bad Sir Cuthbert would have attended the assizes along with at least forty men, gentlemen and serving men. The judges for whom Covell and Halsall waited were two aristocratic gentlemen – Sir Edward Bromley of Snifall Grange, Shropshire (whose beautiful memorial may be viewed in St Peter's church, Warfield)[29] and Sir James Altham of Oxhey Place, Hertfordshire. Accompanying them was a man of tantamount importance to our knowledge of the Lancashire witches – the Associate Clerk of Assize, Thomas Potts.

Without his book, *The Wonderfull Discoverie of Witches in the Countie of Lancaster*,[30] published in 1613, very little would be known today about Demdike, Chattox and the rest – there were probably only a couple of brief and occasional references to them in other sources. For various reasons the judges instructed Potts to provide a commentary on the witch trial. Unfortunately space decrees that we cannot analyse here the motivation behind this important work.[31] Suffice it to say that we must constantly bear in mind that Potts and his masters had their own agenda, and the work might very well contain some deliberate propaganda and misinformation, along with numerous omissions and inaccuracies.[32] There were few people left in any position or with any inclination to argue with his portrayal of the witches' trials once they were over with.

The great spectacle that was the Court of Assize commenced on Monday 17th August and the trials of the witches kicked off on the following day.[33] As P. G. Lawson puts it, 'Each stage of a sitting of the assizes had about it a theatrical quality, from the ceremonial arrival of the judges at the borders of the county, to their procession into court, and finally to that solemn moment when the presiding judge pronounced the death sentence.'[34] The poor unfortunates from Pendle must have been highly intimidated by the proceedings and very confused when they were eventually dragged into the courtroom[35] to be confronted by Roger Nowell as prosecutor.

'Trial of Witches 1612' as imagined by Fred Kirk Shaw in 1913
(Reproduced courtesy of Lancashire County Museum Service)

Those accused of crimes at the assizes did not receive individual trials, but were tried in groups – often up to seven at a time – in rapid succession. With the general hubbub in the courtroom and the great number of accused with which they had to deal, this could result in the jurymen confusing evidence against different prisoners.[36] It is not clear how much time was taken up each day by the proceedings against the witches. The courts could sit from seven o'clock in the morning until eleven o'clock at night, and many other trials apart from those of the witches may well have been packed into those three days.

Whether the accused witches spoke much in court is also uncertain; if they did speak it is most unlikely that the aristocratic judges Bromley and Altham would have understood a word they said. We do know that Elizabeth Device (tried on Tuesday 18th) had plenty to say when Roger Nowell suddenly produced her young daughter Jennet as a prosecution witness, like a rabbit out of a hat.[37] So understandably enraged was she at her daughter's public betrayal of her family that she had to be dragged out of court yelling abuse, and it is difficult to blame her. The next day poor Alizon was removed from her group of prisoners to be confronted yet again with her nemesis, the former pedlar John Law. Law seems to have been determined to drum up sympathy and gain some sort of incapacity

DAEMONOLO-

GIE, IN FORME

of a Dialogue,

Diuided into three Bookes.

IN MY DEFENCE GOD ME DEFEND.

EDINBVRGH

Printed by Robert Walde-graue,
Printer to the Kings Majeſtie. An.1597.

Cum Privilegio Regio.

'Daemonologie', by King James I

benefit for his injuries from the local gentry on the occasion of the trial, and in this he was successful.

It is evident that seventeenth-century judges generally condemned to death those defendants whose image (both physical and psychological) rendered them suitable for such a fate. They had to be regarded as appropriate participants in what could be termed the 'ceremony of the gallows'. With her forceful personality (so unseemly in a female!), her lack of dependence on any man (ditto) and the fact that she had a squint, it was always obvious that Elizabeth Device, for example, would never survive any trial by jury as a witch. Deformity had long been associated with witchcraft and those afflicted with a squint, or peculiar eyes generally, were regarded with particular suspicion. Elizabeth would therefore have been considered by the judges as a very suitable candidate to take part in the formalised ritual of death, as would Mother Chattox. Mumbling was also considered a sure indication that the mumbler was a wicked witch.

The condemnation of Alice Nutter in particular has always mystified historians. At first glance she does not seem to fit the bill as a suitable candidate for execution, being of a higher social status than the rest.[38] Alice would, however, have known Mother Demdike well and probably attended Malkin Tower in response to an appeal for support from the Device family. We should perhaps consider that Potts may have used Alice Nutter in an attempt to ensure the Lancashire witches conformed to the ideas of King James as set out in his book *Daemonologie*. The king stated in his book that there were two types of witches – those of high estate and the poorer sort – an idea repeated word for word in Potts' book. Potts may therefore have exaggerated Alice's status as a wealthy woman to make her conform to the status of a witch of 'high estate'. If this is the case, then her condemnation becomes rather less surprising. On the same note, Potts may even have over-emphasised the low status of the other witches in order to make them fit King James' 'witchcraft model'.

The Sentences

By Wednesday 19th August the witch trials had ended. Chattox, along with her daughter Anne Redfearn, Elizabeth Device and her children James Device and Alizon Device, Katherine Hewitt (alias Mouldheels) of Colne, John and Jane Bulcock of Moss End and Alice Nutter of Rough Lee, were all found guilty and sentenced to death by hanging. As a rule, witches were not burned at the stake in England,[39] though they suffered this fate in Scotland where Continental witch

Woodcut of miscreants in the pillory

laws were in force. Also handed the death penalty was poor old Isabel Robey from Windle, St Helens, in spite of the fact there was very little evidence against her. Presumably, she made the mistake of looking and acting like a typical witch.

Margaret Pearson from Padiham, who, according to the trial evidence, seems to have done a lot more witching than Mistress Robey, somehow managed to escape with the lesser sentence of a year's imprisonment and four stints in the pillory. On four market days in Clitheroe, Padiham, Whalley and Lancaster, Margaret had to stand in the pillory wearing a large paper fastened to her head which stated her offence in large letters. Being pilloried was no joke, as the crowd could occasionally turn very nasty indeed, resulting in the death of the person concerned. It seems that the case of Margaret Pearson had mostly been dealt with by Nicholas Bannister of Altham, Roger Nowell's associate magistrate. It may be significant that Bannister died and was buried in Altham church at about the same time the trials were taking place. Without Bannister present in Lancaster to prosecute in person, perhaps the evidence against Pearson seemed rather less persuasive than it might have done had he been present. She may also have been spared because, for some reason, she did not conform to the stereotypical image of a witch.

Those condemned were returned to their cells to prepare for death on the following day.[40] Before they were taken down, Judge Bromley informed them that a 'learned and worthie Preacher' would be on hand to prepare them for the next

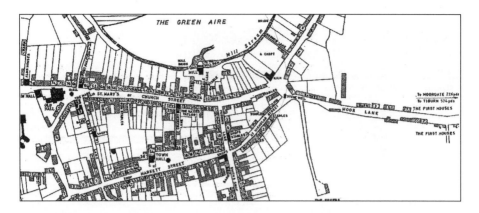

Reconstruction of Lancaster in 1684, from Towneley Map. By Kenneth Docton, 1684 (Reproduced courtesy of Lancaster University)

world. This may have been Mr Leigh of Standish, who is known to have been present.[41] It is impossible to imagine how the Pendle folk must have felt as the sun began to rise on their last day on earth.

The Ritual of Death

Preparation of the condemned for the great 'ceremony of the gallows' on Thursday 20th August 1612 would have started early in the day. The prisoners had their hands pinioned in front of them (to enable prayer) and a noose (or halter) placed around their necks. Chattox, Elizabeth Device and the others were then placed in open carts and probably obliged to sit upon their own coffins. Accompanied by the Sheriff (or under Sheriff), the chaplain, the hangman and an armed guard, the procession began its slow and miserable progress out of the castle. The condemned men and women then retraced the same route by which they had arrived in Lancaster some three months earlier. Travelling east out of the town, they passed Stonegate and entered Moor Lane, this time no doubt lined with a throng of jeering and abusive onlookers. Tradition allowed condemned felons a final drink or two on the way to execution, and the witches may have stopped at the Golden Lion on Moor Lane, or at one of the other ancient inns such as the Cross Keys.

At Gallows Hill, or Tiburn, the procession came to a halt. The location of the gallows is clearly indicated on a map of 1684, which was discovered in the cellar of Towneley Hall in 1952. On the map Moor Lane is marked, along with the 'first houses'. From this point, according to the map, Tiburn was 574 yards further on. To confirm the location, the gallows are marked on Yates' map of 1786 as being located in the angle formed by Quernmore and Wyresdale Road, very close to old quarries. When executions were no longer carried out on the moor, Lancaster built its enlarged workhouse on the site in 1787.[42] It is believed that the actual gallows stood on the spot later occupied by the Master's house.[43]

The gallows at Lancaster were known as 'Tiburn' after the famous Tyburn Tree in London. The name refers to the shape of the gallows, which took the form of a horizontal wooden triangle supported on three legs. Several criminals could be despatched at once on this contraption and it was ideal, therefore, for mass executions such as that of the Lancashire witches on 20th August 1612.

The condemned witches would have been greeted by an enormous and unruly crowd, all of whom considered 'hanging day' an excellent day out, especially when witches were on the menu. Indeed a substantial section of the crowd, which may have numbered thousands, had probably walked all night from the Pendle area to witness the executions. This was certainly the case in 1862, when a murderer from Colne managed to commit suicide in the cell before he could be hanged. Hordes of people who had walked all night from Colne to watch his execution were not best pleased at being denied their prey.[44]

Once the condemned witches had climbed down from the carts, they were expected to play their parts in the spectacle along with the hangman and the chaplain, however perverse we may consider this obligation. As Gregory Durston says, 'In this function, clerics appear to have played a major role in producing almost stereotyped patterns of behaviour at the gallows, manifest in features such as the last dying speeches of the condemned ... Socially, an expression of full contrition might even serve to re-integrate the witch into the community, while establishing a triumph over the devil, and providing a cautionary example of the dangers of witchcraft. It appears that the condemned person often co-operated in this process'.[45]

John and Jane Bulcock were certainly not willing to co-operate in any such process. Potts tells us that they persisted in 'crying out in a very violent and outra-geous manner, even to the gallowes, where they died impenitent for anything we know, because they died silent in the particulars.' [46]

In other words, mother and son vociferously protested their innocence until they got to the gallows, but remained mute and unrepentant when they arrived there, which just wasn't done. Alice Nutter likewise refused to co-operate in the gallows ceremony; instead of giving the required speech of penitence, she

The original Tyburn gallows in London, after which the Lancaster gallows were named "Tiburn"

remained steadfastly silent even *in articulo mortis* (at the point of death). All three must have annoyed the chaplain (either Mr Leigh of Standish or the castle chaplain) very much indeed. Presumably, the rest expressed contrition for their crime. By the time the awful moment arrived, a bleak resignation may have dulled the senses – assisted, hopefully, by a couple of shots of alcohol on the journey. With any luck, poor damaged James Device wouldn't even know what planet he was on. When considering the victims' mental state, we must remember that the condemned men and women did not believe that death was the end of things. As an added torture, they would have fully expected the Devil to drag them off to hell if they did not demonstrate penitence.

Against the gallows a ladder would have been propped. The witches were then obliged to climb the ladder, and the hangman threw the rope over the beam of the gallows. One by one, the Lancashire witches were 'turned off' the ladder and launched into eternity. But I'm afraid none of them would be allowed to plunge into black oblivion instantaneously. Hanging was by no means an easy-option death in those days. The drop involved was usually so short (only a few inches) that there was little if any chance of the neck being broken. If you were very lucky indeed, loss of consciousness could set in after a few moments if the rope happened to cut off the blood supply to the brain. But normally, hanging involved being slowly and painfully strangled due to the weight of the person's own body tightening the noose. The victim would typically struggle violently for about 1–3 minutes. He or she would then jerk around convulsively, though they would not necessarily be conscious by this time. These movements were known as 'dancing the Tyburn jig'. In order to hasten the victim's death, friends and relatives (and sometimes the hangman) might pull on the legs to curtail the suffering.

Although a couple of minutes of being throttled may not sound very long, it must have seemed like an eternity for the person concerned. An Iranian man called Niazali survived a short-drop hanging in Iran in 1996, and described the experience to the newspaper *Kayhan*: 'That first second lasted like a thousand years. I felt my arms and legs jerking out of control. Up on the gallows in the dark, I was trying to fill my lungs with air, but they were crumpled up like plastic bags.'[47] In 1772 Mary Hilton was hanged at Lancaster Tiburn before being burned at the stake for the poisoning of her husband. Mary was hanged for fifteen minutes before being cut down and 'before she was dead was let down into the fire, consisting of faggots and two barrels of tar. She was beginning to move before the fire got hold of her.'[48]

We do not know whether or not hoods were placed over the heads of the condemned witches – often done to hide the physical effects of the execution from the crowd. The result of short-drop hanging on human features was not a pretty one. The face swelled up and the tongue protruded, while the eyes became red and were sometimes partially forced out of their sockets. To make matters worse, a bloody froth or mucus sometimes issued from the lips and nostrils. Certainly not an easy death to suffer or indeed to witness.

No doubt, as the struggles of the condemned witches diminished, the crowd at Lancaster would gradually have fallen silent. It is to be hoped that none of the witches suffered longer than was necessary, and that the hangman pulled on their legs to hasten the proceedings. However, I fear that witches would have received no such mercy.

Burial of the Lancashire Witches

We do not know where the bodies of the Pendle witches (or Isabel Robey) lie buried. As the gallows lay very near to the site of old quarries (now Williamson Park), it is possible that the bodies were buried carelessly and shallowly in rock crevices; this was the method used to dispose of the bodies of the American witches of Salem.[49]

However, it is also feasible that the executed witches were buried in a graveyard. There seems to be a general misconception that witches could not be buried in such a locality. Yet Isabella Rigby – executed for witchcraft on Lancaster Moor in 1666 – was without doubt buried in the graveyard of the Priory Church of St Mary, opposite Lancaster Castle, as her name appears in the burial register.[50] It also seems that no less than sixteen witches may have been buried in the graveyard of St Andrew's church, Newcastle-upon-Tyne,[51] while in nearby Gateshead, the parish books record in 1649: 'Paid at Mrs Watson's when the justices sate to examine the witches, 3s 4d.; paid for a grave for a witch, 6d.; paid for trying the witches, £1 5s.'

It is also recorded in the parish records of St Mary-on-the-Hill, Chester, that in 1656 three witches hanged at the Michaelmas Assizes were buried in the corner by the castle ditch in the churchyard on 8th October.[52] This church was used to bury execution victims from the nearby castle.

Lancaster Castle

The Priory Church, in whose graveyard the Lancashire Witches may be interred

The names of our witches do not appear in the burial record of the Priory church of St Mary for 1612. However, there are many reasons why they might have been omitted. To take an example from Horsham in West Sussex, an entry in the burial register for 1586 records that 'the prysners y't dyed In the Gaole at Horsham this yeare and buryed in ye Churchyarde were not made knowen unto the vicar and therefore not here entered.' It also seems that there were many contemporary statements of the burials of executed felons and alleged felons in the Horsham churchyard, entries of which do not appear in the church registers.[53]

It seems at least possible, therefore, that the Lancashire witches (including Mother Demdike) may very well be buried somewhere in the vicinity of the Priory, probably in a communal pit. As executed felons, they would not have been entitled to a Christian burial, i.e. to any prayers or psalms being recited as they were interred. Perhaps, as tourists saunter around the Priory and castle grounds, they could say a little prayer for the Lancashire witches over whose silent and forgotten remains they might well have unwittingly stepped.

CHAPTER TWO

Dolls of Clay, Fairies and Familiar Spirits

And Now About the Cauldron Sing
Like Elves and Fairies in a Ring ... [1]

evelations of evil-doing by the Pendle witches appeared to provide positive proof to everybody that His Satanic Majesty was abroad in England and was engaged in an active recruitment drive. Satan seemed to have a particular penchant for enrolling Lancashire folk in his infernal army. As far away as London, Pendle Forest would soon gain an evil reputation as a notorious witchcraft hotspot, while the Romany people came to associate the county exclusively with magic and eventually named Lancashire *Chohawniskey tem*, meaning 'Witches' Country'.[2] Predictably, Lancastrians became increasingly paranoid about the possibility of fresh batches of evil hags hatching out in their midst.

In the wake of the trial and execution of so many condemned witches, the fear of malevolent magic was seen to be a completely justified one. This legacy of fear bequeathed by the witches of 1612 provided the inspiration for many future witchcraft accusations in Lancashire and further afield.

Indeed, such was the level of alarm generated by Demdike, Chattox and their respective broods, that their very names soon became synonymous and even interchangeable with the word 'witch'. 'Anne, thou art a Chadwick and a Demdike,' said Richard Sharples of Clitheroe in 1626, as he accused his neighbour Anne Waine of witchcraft.[3] Similarly, Dorothy Shawe of Skippoole complained a year later that William Wilkinson had slandered her by threatening: 'Thou art a

witch and a Demdyke, God Blesse me from all Witches, I am affrayd of my wife, children, and goods, and thou shall knowe yt.'[4]

The intensity of horror inspired by 'black' witches (as opposed to wise-men and women, or 'white witches') in the seventeenth century should never be underestimated by the modern reader. There seems to be little, if any, evidence that any of these individuals were regarded by their contemporaries as herb-gathering, nature-loving pagans who had somehow been 'left over' from an 'Old Religion'. Make no mistake, black witches were regarded as malevolent servants of Satan, and even white witches were beheld with a degree of mistrust. It is difficult in this day and age to take seriously the idea of someone making a pact with the Devil, but by the time the Pendle witches lived and died, the satanic pact had been accepted as a complete reality, even by the majority of educated people. Whether or not we accept these ideas today is entirely irrelevant.

Witches were considered to have sold their souls to Satan in exchange for receiving the power to work *maleficia*. Originally this word just meant 'wrong-doing'. Eventually, however, it came to mean 'malevolent sorcery', usually involving murder or injury to other people and the destruction of livestock. The witches and their familiar spirits were considered by their seventeenth-century contemporaries as a secret satanic army, capable of the most revolting barbarities including cannibalism and child murder. When trying to imagine how seventeenth-century people regarded witches, think *Blair Witch*, *Coffin Rock* and eviscerated bodies, rather than cute, twitchy-nosed Samantha of *Bewitched*!

The Art of the 'Voodoo Doll', aka Picture of Clay

Of what sort of evil spells, then, were Lancastrians so afraid? The dreaded *maleficia* could take many forms – from supernatural murder or injury to people and animals, to general bad luck generated by the casting of the evil eye. In her confession to Roger Nowell, Mother Demdike described one of the most famous and well-documented methods of committing murder by black magic:

> And further this Examinate confesseth, and sayth, that the speediest way to take a mans life away by Witchcraft, is to make a Picture of Clay, like unto the shape of the person whom they meane to kill, & dry it thorowly: and when they would haue them to be ill in any one place more then an other; then take a Thorne or Pinne, and pricke it in that part of the Picture you would so haue to be ill; and when you would haue any part of the Body to consume away, then take that part of the Picture, and burne it. And when they would haue the whole body to consume away, then take the remnant of the sayd Picture, and burne it: and so thereupon by that meanes, the body shall die.[5]

The image of a witch sticking pins into a doll made to resemble her victim (these days somewhat inaccurately (but conveniently) referred to by the blanket term 'voodoo doll') is so famous that it is almost a cliché. This form of sympathetic image magic (based on the assumption that a person or thing can be supernaturally affected through its name or an object representing it) is extremely ancient. We are told in ancient Egyptian magical texts that figurines were thought to be more effective if they incorporated something from the intended victim. This could include items such as hair, nail-clippings or bodily fluids. A recent find from Piazza Euclid in Rome turned up the remains of lead curses and seven voodoo

Witches offering 'Voodoo Dolls' to the Devil for his approval

dolls. These came to light embedded in the mud surrounding the remains of the holding tank of an ancient Roman fountain dedicated to a minor goddess Anna Perenna. The dolls were fashioned out of various materials including wax and flour, and were enclosed within lead canisters. (Lead has always been a material associated with ill-wishing and cursing.) They are thought to date from the fourth century AD and to be the work of a professional Roman witch.[6]

Moving forward in time, and closer to home, in 1560 the court of Queen Elizabeth was buzzing with news of the discovery of a wax image of the Queen. It came to light at Lincoln's Inn and had a pin jabbed through its chest.[7] More significantly, perhaps, the witches of North Berwick had also made an attempt on the life of James I by sticking pins into his image. According to one of the accused witches – the young schoolmaster John Cunningham (or Doctor Fian) – they met with the Devil near Prestonpans, and the wax image, wrapped in a cloth, was shown to his Infernal Majesty. When he had approved it, the witches passed it from hand to hand saying, 'This is King James the Sixth, ordained to be consumed at the instance of a nobleman Francis, Earl Bothwell.' We should remember that torture was legal in Scotland and Fian's confession no doubt had a lot to do with his fingernails being ripped out with pincers, and needles being rammed into the exposed raw flesh.[8] However, in view of poor Fian's evidence, the king would naturally be very much interested in any other examples of image magic which came to light in contemporary witchcraft trials.

The Pendle Witches and Pictures of Clay

The making of voodoo dolls (called 'clay pictures' by the Lancashire witches) seems to have been a technique frequently practised by local sorceresses when they wished to rid themselves of an enemy. This wealth of evidence may of course be the result of leading questions asked during the investigations. King James' experiences with the Scottish witches was well known, and Roger Nowell might well have asked eagerly and specifically about the use of this sort of magic. Be that as it may, according to Thomas Potts, the most skilled or 'cunning' at fashioning a picture of clay was Anne Redfearn.[9]

He tells us that all men who knew her affirmed that she was more dangerous than her mother 'for she made all or most of the Pictures of Clay that were made or found at any time.' Anne and her mother Chattox were accused of making pictures of Christopher, Robert and Marie Nutter.[10] Alizon Device also described how she had seen Chattox sitting in her garden with a clay figure that

Mother Chattox asking the Sexton to bury a clay image in the graveyard of Newchurch-in-Pendle (Sir John Gilbert, 1854)

she attempted to hide in her apron. (It is difficult to decide who is the less stealthy in this story –Alizon for not managing to sneak up on Chattox unobserved, or Chattox for failing miserably to conceal the image from Alizon!) When Alizon mentioned the incident to her mother, Elizabeth ventured the opinion that this figure represented a child of John Moore's, who later died.[11]

James Device and his mother Elizabeth provided us with a detailed description of their method of fashioning pictures to commit magical murder. In 1608/9, Elizabeth's familiar spirit Ball told her to make a picture of John Robinson, alias Swyer. Robinson had made the mistake of accusing Elizabeth Device of having a bastard child with a man called Sellar. Elizabeth would naturally be keen to take swift revenge for this attack on her virtue. She collected clay from the west end of her house, made the image and then brought it into the house where she dried it for two days. Elizabeth then began to crumble it away and continued to do so bit by bit, every day for about three weeks. Within two days of the picture being crumbled away to nothing, we are told that John Robinson was dead.[12]

One of the strangest stories told about a clay doll also involves the theft of some teeth from the graveyard of St Mary's church in the village of Newchurch-in-Pendle. James Device told magistrates Roger Nowell and Nicholas Bannister that in about 1600, Anne Chattox removed some teeth from three 'scalpes' (skulls) that had been 'cast out of' a grave. He was not suggesting that Chattox had personally dug up human remains. Burials were often disturbed during the excavation of a new grave, and it was from such an exposed burial that Chattox removed the teeth. This need not be as sinister as it sounds;[13] teeth from skulls were a well-known folk remedy for toothache. In 1666, John Aubrey commented, 'I remember at Bristow (when I was a boy) it was a common fashion for the woemen, to get a Tooth out of a sckhull in ye ch:yard, wch they wore as a preservative against the Tooth-ach'.[14] Similar remedies persisted well into the nineteenth century. Other Pendle folk as well as Chattox may have helped themselves to a few teeth from the Newchurch grave, but in the context of a witchcraft trial any mention of human remains would be interpreted in a sinister light.[15]

Chattox took eight teeth, keeping four for herself and giving the other four to Demdike. The two were presumably still on friendly terms at this time, and it was probably an act of kindness on Chattox's part to share the ingredients of her toothache remedy with Demdike. Both of them lived in an age, and were of an age, when toothache was a chronic and agonising problem.

We should note that nowhere is it suggested that the Lancashire witches of 1612 stuck pins into the images they made. This may be because all their pictures of clay were made with the intention of killing the victims rather than injuring them. Neither, as far as we know, did the Lancashire witches incorporate hair or other personal substances into the fabric of the clay doll in order to identify it with the victim.

The crumbling technique used by both James and Elizabeth Device differs from that described by Demdike. Her method of burning the doll instead resembles the description in James I's *Daemonologie*[16] rather than the methods allegedly employed by her own family. This is extremely suspicious. It is more than likely that Thomas Potts was deliberately attempting to mislead his readers into thinking that Demdike had confessed to performing this magical act herself. Certainly this is how many modern sources interpret the information. In fact, there seems to be little doubt that she was merely repeating the description of a practice she had heard about (or possibly had read out loud to her).

The size of the clay images allegedly fashioned by the Redfearn family (according to James Device) is also remarkable. At around eighteen inches long, they used quite substantial lumps of clay. We tend to imagine the archetypal

The author and the late Cecil Williamson examine Voodoo dolls at
Mr Williamson's Witchcraft Museum in Cornwall, 1991

witch holding a little doll in one hand while sticking pins into it with the other. These witches seem to have made a different type of image altogether. We might also notice that the west end of the house seems to have had some magical significance (which is not currently understood) in the production and burial of such images.

Publishing Demdike's 'instructions' on 'the speediest way to take a man's life away by witchcraft', along with the general publicity given to the above practice by Thomas Potts in his *Wonderfull Discoverie*, must have terrified his readers out of their wits. It must also have helped to fix in the general public's mind once and for all the association between witches and supernatural murder by voodoo doll. It does not really matter whether or not the witches actually practised image magic or not. The important thing to understand is that the people of the time *thought* that they did. The result was that fear generated by this sort of *maleficia* continued through the years and is still capable of causing consternation in the twenty-first century. It is with the written and physical evidence created by this fear that we are primarily concerned.

In his 1888 book *Pendle Hill in History and Literature*, James McKay commented that, 'Clay or wax images pierced through with pins and needles are occasionally met with in churchyards and gardens where they have been placed for the purpose of causing the death of the person they represent.' [17] And in 1900 we are told that some workmen altering a fireplace at Crow Trees Cottage in Worston, near Clitheroe, received a very nasty shock. To their horror a clay image of a monk, stuck full of pins, tumbled down on them. It was thought at the time that it was a representation of John Paslew, the last abbot of Whalley Abbey. Unfortunately, so goes the story, the men smashed it up in terror which is a great pity.[18] Regrettably I remain far from convinced that this clay image was a genuine relic of the practice of *maleficia* – if indeed the artefact ever existed at all. For in Harrison Ainsworth's famous Gothic novel *The Lancashire Witches* we find an enlightening passage:

> 'Let me hear them and I will judge,' said Paslew. Thus urged the monk went on:
> 'One shall sit at a solemn feast,
> Half warrior, half priest,
> The greatest there shall be the least.'
> 'The last verse,' observed the monk 'has been added to the ditty by Nicholas Demdike. I heard him sing it the other day at the abbey gate.'
> 'What, Nicholas Demdike of Worston?' cried the abbot; 'he whose wife is a witch?'
> 'The same,' replied Eastgate.[19]

I very much suspect that Harrison Ainsworth's reference to Nicholas and Bess Demdike living at Worston may have inspired one of the men working on this seventeenth-century listed cottage to play a nasty trick on a mate by having the doll fall down on him. Personal experience has also taught me that people are notoriously prone to confusing events described in romantic Victorian novels with historical fact. There being no evidence that Demdike's mother or any other witch ever lived in Worston, this dramatic discovery of a relic of witchcraft there, is, to put it mildly, very suspicious.

Voodoo dolls of all descriptions continue to be produced and to inspire dread in those of a superstitious and credulous frame of mind. An excellent modern selection may be viewed at the Museum of Witchcraft in Boscastle, Cornwall.

Before we leave the subject, it should be noted that dolls could occasionally be deployed to protect and heal, as well as to harm. The same is true in the Voodoo religion and modern Wicca. Peering out of a display case in Touchstones Museum, Rochdale, is a large and fascinating doll manufactured out of red wax. Dating probably from the nineteenth century, it is said to have been placed in the sickroom of children to ward off disease and evil spirits. I am not aware of any similar examples.

Another artefact sometimes discovered in old houses and barns also has a somewhat ambiguous role in magic. Animal hearts pierced over and over again with nails and pins could occasionally be used in *maleficia*. According to *Folklore of the Northern Counties of England* (1879), residing in a village near Preston, there was a girl who 'when slighted by her lover, got a hare's heart, stuck it full of pins, and buried it with many imprecations against the faithless man, whom she hoped by these means to torment'.[20] Although we have no record of the Lancashire witches employing this charm it is likely that they were both aware of its various uses and employed it themselves.

Some Lancastrians have been horrified to find an example of this macabre form of sympathetic magic on their property. One of these grisly relics was found in a house in Burnley in the 1970s,[21] and another example is held in the social history collections of Cliffe Castle Museum, Keighley. These transfixed hearts (and occasionally onions) seem to have been used both to protect bewitched cattle and to reveal the identity of unknown witches; in reality this type of magic is similar in function to that of a witch bottle. J. D. Lang says, 'A farmer complained his cattle had been overlooked and were all gradually dying off. He was told to take the heart out of the last animal that had died and push the heart, stuck all over with pins and nails, up the chimney so that the overlooking would pass back again where it had come from'.[22]

A heart stuck with pins

Farmers were from time to time advised to take more drastic action and told to burn the heart over a hot fire. This would force the witch to appear – presumably because the heart represented the witch, who could feel herself burning – and the sorceress might then be 'persuaded' to remove her spell from the cattle.

Occasionally, a farmer would resort to even more extreme measures and would burn an animal alive, often on the advice of the local wise-man. This nauseating ceremony certainly took place in Lancashire. In the pamphlet 'Lancashire Witchcraft Charms and Spells', authors John Harland and Thomas Turner Wilkinson comment, 'Another individual, well known to the writer, was so far convinced that certain casualties that happened to his cattle arose from the practice of witchcraft, that he unconsciously resorted to Baal worship and consumed a live calf in the fire, in order to counteract the influences of his unknown enemies.'[23]

Fortunately, things usually had to be very bad indeed before someone consulted a wise-man. In the aftermath of the 1612 trials, folk would certainly have redoubled their personal efforts to protect themselves from *maleficia*. Before going to the expense of paying for the professional help of the white witches, other avenues could be explored. Lancastrians had access to a rich storehouse of folk remedies against witchcraft, which had been tried and tested over the centuries. These traditional remedies continued to be employed against malevolent magic into living memory, and some still try them today.

One of the main worries of the householder was that the witch might gain entry to the home and to the farm buildings, and every vulnerable spot in these buildings must therefore be fortified against both the witch and her familiar spirit. A very popular defence still well known today (although it has degenerated into a mere good luck charm), is the practice of nailing a horseshoe over the door.

Cold Iron, Familiars and Fairies

Horseshoes have been considered lucky amulets for many hundreds of years. An early reference from the late fourteenth century says that, ' ... horseshoes ... are among the luckiest finds ...' and in 1507 the '*Gospelles of Dystaves*' say that, 'He yt fyndeth a horse shoo or a pece of one, he shall haue good fortune'.[24] Opinion differed and differs still as to which way up the horseshoe should be hung . Some say that the heels should be upward in a cup formation so that the luck doesn't run out, while others prefer the heels to point downwards to allow luck to flow out to everyone. According to tradition, a horseshoe had to be found by chance on the road, and it was considered even more efficacious if some original nails remained in it.

By the late sixteenth century, rather than just being considered lucky, horseshoes were being used specifically as *apotropaic* (protective) devices designed to prevent witches and their familiar spirits from entering buildings. In 1584, Reginald Scot's *Discoverie of Witchcraft* advised us, 'To prevent and cure all mischeefs wrought by these charmes & witchcrafts ... naile a horse shoe at the inside of the outmost threshold of your house, and so you shall be sure that no witch shall have power to enter ... You shall find that rule observed in manie countrie houses'.[25]

Illustration by George Cruikshank, 1871

The origin of the belief that a horseshoe repelled witches is a matter for debate. Metals were considered to have magical properties, and the iron out of which horseshoes were forged was considered especially potent. This conviction that supernatural entities were repelled by 'cold iron' probably had a very early origin indeed, possibly dating from when iron was a new, rare and mysterious metal.

The Fay

Domestic and farm buildings were protected by iron long before the great witch scares of the sixteenth and seventeenth centuries. Before witches were press-ganged into their role of bogeywomen-in-chief, Lancastrians were apprehensive about an equally, if not more, alarming supernatural threat. These magical menaces, which had to be denied access to houses and farm buildings at all costs, were given many names. Most people today know them as fairies or elves (the latter being the older term), but they are also referred to as the 'fair folk', the 'good neighbours', and the 'fay'. In Ireland they were known as *sidhe* (pronounced 'shee') and in Scotland, *Danoine Sith*.

Woodcut of the fay inside a hill

Readers should immediately disabuse themselves of the mistaken idea that early modern fairies were cute and sweet. Fairies were scary in the old days. They did not sit about in cowslips fluttering their wings and eyelashes – at least they might do so, but that would be just before they went for your throat. Fairies had the potential to be extremely malignant. Some liked nothing more than to spread disease, steal human babies, kidnap adults, shoot animals with their elf shot, tangle human hair and animal manes into knotted 'elf locks' and ride animals all night long so they collapsed in exhaustion.

Even in the early twentieth century, boys in Scotland and in the north of England were dressed as girls until the age of five. This was to fool the fairies who might otherwise steal the boy child to serve in their fairy armies. A photograph of my father as a toddler in 1918, wearing a fetching little dress, demonstrates this practice beyond a doubt. Water fairies such as Jenny Greenteeth, Peg o' Nell and Peg Powler took a grim delight in drowning the unwary as they dragged them to the bottom of rivers, pools and wells.

The Other Peg

Peg o' Nell, who lurks menacingly in the River Ribble at Brungerley just outside Clitheroe, is a particularly hungry water spirit that demands an animal or human sacrifice every seven years on a particular night known as Peg's Night. The next one is due at Christmas 2013.

She has been rationalised as the ghost of a servant girl who died at the hands of her mistress at Waddow Hall many years ago, but there seems little doubt that this tale preserves the memory of a malignant local water fairy or deity. A well by the River Ribble in the grounds of Waddow Hall is presided over by the headless statue of Peg. The missing head is, according to some reports, kept in an upper room of the hall. In reality the statue is that of a saint, which in all likelihood was beheaded by Protestants during the sixteenth or seventeenth century. It probably stood originally in a private chapel in Waddow Hall that was owned by the Tempests, a leading Roman Catholic family of the area.

Peg's legend may have arisen as a result of the reputation of the Hipping Stones at Brungerley. These were large stepping stones, about 55 in all, set at an acute angle across the river and a few yards upstream from the present bridge. It was upon these stones that King Henry VI was captured during the Wars of the Roses. Providing the only means of getting across the river at Brungerley until

Medieval wooden statue known as
Peg o' Nell, at Brungerley Farm,
near Clitheroe

the present bridge was built in 1816, this was a notoriously treacherous crossing place and resulted in many fatalities by drowning over the years.

The legend of Peg o' Nell and her headless statue at Waddow is fairly well known in Northern folklore, but there is another Peg that is less famous. This Peg lives in a barn at Brungerley Farm, on the rising ground above the site of the Hipping Stones. She is a wooden statue – probably medieval – and is holding in her arms a paschal lamb. About 33 inches tall, Peg is mounted upon one of the walls of the upper floor of the shippen. Her condition has deteriorated badly in recent years as she was partially burnt in a fire in about 1984.

Brungerley Farm dates back to the late eighteenth century, and has been occupied by the Berry family for four generations. Mr Berry, who introduced me to Peg on 9th August 2010, is in his seventies, but made me feel at least one hundred and seventy years old. In order to view the statue it was necessary to clamber up to the first storey of the barn by way of a vertical stepladder and through a trap door. Mr Berry clambered up the ladder in a sprightly fashion, putting me in mind of a super-fit Olympic athlete. I wheezed, coughed and stumbled miserably after him, thinking every breath was going to be my last. However, it was well worth the climb to meet this fascinating lady, who has been protecting the animals in the barn as long as anyone can remember. According to Mr Berry, the medieval statue has always been known as Peg o' Nell, so here we have a rather curious contradiction. While Peg o' Nell the malignant water fairy squats hungrily in the River Ribble waiting to drag down the unwary into the depths, another Peg sits benevolently in

A A Witch   B A Spirit raised by the Witch
C A Friar raising his Imps.   D A Fairy Ring.
E A Witch rideing on the Devill through the Aire
F An Inchanted Castle

Woodcut illustrating the close association between fairy, witch and familiar (From Pandaemonium, 1684)

a nearby barn protecting the cattle from witches and evil spirits. It may be that here we have a manifestation of the dual nature of many fay folk/Celtic water goddesses that sometimes play a protective and good-natured role, yet at other times can be vengeful, capricious and hungry for sacrifice.[26]

It is of course most unlikely that people ceased to fear the fair folk just because Demdike and Chattox had grabbed centre stage. There are many similarities between the fears expressed about the fay and those about witches; very often their perceived actions were remarkably similar. Fairies and witches were both said to cast spells and use charms to heal, foresee the future, and dance in circles. In medieval times dancing in a circle was customary. The medieval carol was a circular dance accompanied by music from a harp, pipe and tabor. It could get distinctly boisterous and was extremely unpopular with the church authorities. A fit dance, then, for witches and fairies. By the seventeenth century, circle-dancing was considered not only old-fashioned but abnormal, weird and associated firmly with occult beings.[27] In one old woodcut portraying fairies dancing in a circle, the female fay wear pointed hats and are virtually indistin-guishable from witches.

In common with witches, fairies were also thought have commerce with the Devil, shape-shift, steal unbaptised children, ride horses to exhaustion at night, and both were repelled by iron. Beliefs held regarding the powers of fairies and witches were almost interchangeable. It is not surprising therefore that iron was deployed to deal with both.

Various theories have been offered about the true nature of the creatures known as the fay. Some said they were spirits of the dead, others elemental spirits. Still others thought they were fallen angels or demons, or even pagan gods. Victorian folklorists were of the opinion that fairies were an indigenous Bronze Age people who went into hiding when the 'people of iron' invaded the land. There was also the idea that if you knew the name of a particular fairy, then you could summon it and make it do your bidding. This is reminiscent of the concept of the witch commanding her familiar spirit to carry out magical errands for her. Indeed the similarity is so marked that we might even speculate that the familiars of the witches and the fairy folk were often deemed one and the same. It may also be relevant that in *Daemonologie*, King James I describes Diana as both Goddess of the Witches and the Queen of Phairie, and classes 'the fairie' as one of the classes of evil spirits which may be controlled by witches.[28]

In a very early text concerning the fair folk called *The Secret Commonwealth of Elves, Fauns and Fairies* (1691), Scottish clergyman Robert Kirk seems to emphasise this probable link between the witch and the fairy: 'The Tabhaisver, or Seer, that corresponds with this kind of Familiars, can bring them with a Spel to appear to himself or others when he pleases, as readily as Endor Witch to those of her Kind. He tells, they are ever readiest to go on hurtfull Errands, but seldom will be the Messengers of great Good to Men'.[29]

It is not therefore surprising that iron continued to be utilised to repel both the fairy and familiar spirit of the witch because all the evidence points to them being thought of as the same thing by both the witch and the general public. This strange and ambivalent role played by fairies is demonstrated by a slander case heard in Manchester in 1601 when Christopher Prestwick objected vigorously to Margaret Chetham accusing him of 'selling his soul to the fairies' (not, we note, to Satan).[30]

Tibb, Ball and the Familiars of the Pendle Witches

When we think of a witch's familiar we always tend to think of the archetypal black cat. However, the familiar spirits of the Pendle witches were, with one exception, a pretty versatile bunch of shape-shifters. Mother Demdike's familiar was called Tibb. When Demdike first met him at a stonepit near Goldshaw (traditionally Faugh's Quarry on Well Head Road, Newchurch-in-Pendle) he appeared in the form of a boy dressed in a coat that was half brown and half black. On other occasions he appeared as a brown dog, a black cat, a hare and, according to Chattox, as a spotted bitch. Demdike's familiar didn't take orders from her. Quite the opposite, in fact. When she refused to join Chattox and Anne Redfearn in making clay pictures, Tibb shoved her into a ditch and spilt the milk she was carrying.[31]

Tibb insisted on sucking blood from Demdike's side as one part of their bargain, the other being that she gave him her soul. It is interesting to note that there is some evidence to suggest that fairies were also reputed to suck the blood of humans and Demdike tells us in her confession that after Tibb had sucked at her side, it remained blue for several months – rather like a bruise, in fact. This seems reminiscent of the blue bruises left by fairies that often pinched unwary humans, leaving similar blue marks. In return for Demdike's soul and blood, we are led to believe that Tibb disposed of Baldwin the miller's daughter, but his method of doing so is unclear. Also reinforcing the concept of the fairy familiar[32] is the fact that Tibb, along with Ball (the familiar of Elizabeth Device) are both documented fairy names.

Mother Chattox changed her story about her familiar spirit Fancie during the course of the 1612 witchcraft investigations. At her examination at Fence by Roger Nowell on 2nd April, Chattox said that she met her familiar in the shape of a man for the first time at her own home.[33] However, after her rival – Demdike – died in prison, Chattox decided to create a much more exciting story. She blamed Demdike for everything, including persuading her to become a witch against her will.

She now claimed that she had met Fancie for the first time at Malkin Tower where he and Demdike's familiar, Tibb, had provided a wonderful feast for the two witches. Chattox commented that the food did not fill them up or make them feel better.

It is suggestive that this later, more elaborate tale was extracted from Chattox when she was a prisoner in Lancaster Castle on 19th May.[34] Her three interrogators, including the forbidding Thomas Covell, may have been less than gentle.

They probably asked leading questions that were different from those put to her by Roger Nowell and which were designed to extract further incriminating information from the old lady. Covell, Sands and Anderton had probably read all the right books on witchcraft and the 'banquet' described by Chattox suggests that the interrogators had formulated questions having read Nicolas Remy's book *Demonolatry*. In this book we are told 'that the food placed before witches at their Banquets is Tasteless and Mean, and not of a Kind to Satisfy Hunger'.[35] Remy was an avid witch hunter in his capacity of Lord High Justice General of the Duchy of Lorraine from 1591 to 1606.

Predictably, these three powerful men seem to have thoroughly befuddled poor Chattox. At one point in her confession she claimed that Tibb and Fancie were female entities, and that they were both 'shee Spirites, and Diuels'.[36]

James Device had a very active and accommodating familiar spirit called Dandy. Dandy was 'a thing like a brown dog' but he could also appear as a black dog which isn't much of a tribute to the imagination of either the witch or his familiar spirit! They first met 'hard by the new Church in Pendle' when Dandy asked James to give him his soul. Interestingly, Dandy does not appear to have requested a tribute of blood from James. This may have been because their deal was never fully struck and therefore Dandy was not officially entitled to suck blood from James. Alternatively it may suggest that his interrogators thought this practice did not apply to male witches and for this reason did not press him for information on this particular point.[37]

The last time James saw his familiar was just before his arrest. Upon James resolutely refusing to give up his soul unreservedly, Dandy let forth a shriek of rage and disappeared in a dramatic flash of fire. The name of James' familiar may possibly have some connection with the Devil's Dandy Dogs, which were demon dogs of the Cornish Wild Hunt. These dogs hunted for human souls, and breathed fire. Whether or not James would have been aware of Cornish legends is, of course, open to question.

John Duckworth of the Laund is perhaps the most interesting victim of James and his spirit Dandy because of the process involved in killing him. Duckworth had promised James an old shirt (probably as part or full payment for some labouring work he had undertaken). When James went to collect it, Duckworth refused to give it to him. As James was leaving the house, presumably in a fine old temper, Dandy appeared and commented that James had touched the said Duckworth, which gave Dandy power over him. Whereupon James *joined with his spirit*, and asked him to kill Duckworth, who was obligingly dead within a week. This merging of the will of James with that of his familiar is an interesting concept and might suggest that the spirit of the witch accompanied the familiar spirit to carry out *maleficia*.[38]

The last things people wanted getting into their houses and frolicking about in their barns was a couple of marauding fairy/witch spirits. No doubt horseshoes would be hurriedly placed in any vulnerable spot, especially in the areas where the Lancashire witches had been physically present. One of these locations, where horseshoes are still very much in evidence, is Bull Hole Farm, near Newchurch-in-Pendle. The farmer of this property was particularly unlucky in that his family clashed with not just Demdike, but Chattox as well.

The Bulhof

Bull Hole Farm has a curious name. The discovery of a circular structure close by (reburied by the farmer in case it turned out to be Malkin Tower) may represent the remains of some other sort of building, rather than the remains of the Demdike home. For there is an extremely interesting potential origin for the name Bull Hole. The first reference I have come across appears in the Court Rolls of Clitheroe in 1539, in which it is not referred to as Bull Hole but as the far more suggestive 'Bulhof'.[39] This may indicate that the area conceals the remains of a pagan sacred site; *hof* being an old Norse term for temple.

Excavation of such a hof at Hofstadir in Iceland revealed the bones of numerous cattle which had been sacrificed to the gods. They had been slaughtered in a most extraordinary manner in that they were struck heavily between the eyes. This would apparently have caused a veritable fountain of blood to spurt from the animals' heads. Cattle skulls dating from about 1000 AD came to light in both wall and roof debris, suggesting they may have been displayed (or possibly walled up) in these locations.[40] For our purposes, what is of great interest here is that the vast majority of the sacrificed animals at this site appear

Woodcut showing Hofstadir, Iceland. Note the sacred well to the right of the temple with the head of a human sacrifice poking out!

to have been bulls. This is of course extremely suggestive when we consider the name 'Bulhof'.

The bull is an attribute of the god Thor, and was a popular sacrificial animal among the Norsemen. It is therefore an attractive (if extremely speculative) suggestion that the remains of a Viking temple-farm site awaits discovery beneath the earth in the vicinity of Bull Hole Farm. It is also worth pointing out that if a vague memory of a pagan site persisted here into the sixteenth and seventeenth centuries, then this spot may already have acquired a rather sinister and mysterious reputation even before its association with Demdike and Chattox. Old pagan sites were often considered to be haunted places of ill-repute, frequented by fairies and other disreputable supernatural entities.

The Unfortunate John Nutter of Bull Hole

According to Alizon Device, John Nutter had his first unfortunate encounter with the supernatural in about 1606. It is a strange tale. She tells us that Elizabeth, a daughter of Chattox, had managed to beg a dish of milk from the farm. She then carried the dish to a field adjoining Bull Hole where Chattox was waiting for her. Chattox took the milk and transferred it to a can. She then settled down to churn the milk, using two sticks placed across the can. (The actual word used by Potts is *charne*, which should surely be understood as 'churn', rather than 'charm' as others have interpreted it.) Whatever she was doing, John Nutter's son took exception to it and ran over to the field and kicked over the can and the milk.[41] It has to be said that attempting to churn milk into butter in the middle of a field was an odd thing to do. Chattox possibly considered butter much easier to carry back home than a dish of milk. Be that as it may, Nutter's son probably interpreted her actions as an act designed to threaten the health and productivity of his father's cows. We have to remember that Chattox was accused of souring James Robinson's ale simply by tasting it! According to her own confession Chattox had also sent Fancie to bite one of John Moore's brown cows on the head, send it mad and kill it. John Nutter fared no better than John Moore. The morning after the milk churning incident, one of his cows fell sick, languished three or four days and then died.

Not surprisingly, the next time one of his cows fell sick it was to Demdike that the farmer turned for help. This demonstrates that at least some of the locals regarded her as a wise-woman rather than as a satanic witch. Demdike agreed to do her best and Alizon tells us that she led her grandmother out of Malkin Tower

Ruins of the barn at Bull Hole Farm, where Demdike attempted to cure a cow

at ten o'clock at night and left her out by herself for half an hour. Unfortunately Alizon does not tell us where she took her blind old granny or what she did when she was out. It seems to have been normal practice for the wise-woman to treat a sick animal in person, and she also needed to know its name. It is possible, therefore, that Alizon took Demdike to the Bull Hole and left her there. As we have seen, there is a theory that Malkin Tower was only about 500 yards away. Be that as it may, half an hour later little Jennet was dispatched to bring her grandma home.[42]

Unfortunately, news arrived the next morning that the cow had died during the night – an absolute disaster for any farmer.[43] Alizon appears to have offered her opinion to Roger Nowell that Demdike had bewitched the cow to death instead of healing it. With a granddaughter like that, who needed enemies, you might very well ask. However, Alizon should perhaps be given the benefit of the doubt as it is possible that during her interrogation Nowell said to her, 'And do you believe your grandmother bewitched it to death?'. Alizon might then have replied with a shrug or said something like 'maybe'. Nowell would have then felt entirely justified in setting down the statement that Alizon truly believed that Demdike had killed the cow by witchcraft.

According to statements given by Alizon Device, then, poor John Nutter was unfortunate enough to have lost two cows to the *maleficia* of the two most powerful witches in the Forest of Pendle. He does not seem to have given evidence at the Lancaster Assizes, or if he did, Thomas Potts did not see fit to record it.

Many accusations of witchcraft hang on the bewitching of cattle, because these beasts were, of course, extremely important to the livelihood of local farmers. Many of the illnesses attributed to *maleficia* can probably be blamed on poorly-informed or careless husbandry. John Nutter's two cows (along with other livestock which fell prey to 'witchcraft') may, for example, have eaten poisonous plants. These include tall fescue grass, turnip tops, thistle, belladonna and St John's Wort. The latter plant causes the animal to act as though it is demented, and we are often told that a bewitched animal 'went mad' before it died. Unfortunately, St John's Wort was a very popular and common plant in the seventeenth century as it was thought to repel witches and evil spirits! Other perfectly natural reasons for cattle death attributed to witchcraft might be murrain (any disease resembling a plague which led to death), old age and calving complications. During the period of the witch scares, cattle were often weak and vulnerable to disease at the best of times, in part because in the sixteenth and seventeenth centuries dairy cattle were considered better thin than fat. Fat cows supposedly had poor milk flow and so their food rations were kept purposely meagre.[44]

Old horseshoe still protecting the back door of Bull Hole farmhouse

Puck's Well in the field above Bull Hole Farm

Identifiable local sites so closely and reliably associated with both Chattox and Demdike are few and far between. Today, Bull Hole farmhouse, which probably contains elements of the seventeenth-century structure, is a delightful private dwelling which has been sympathetically renovated. It remains, however, a building extremely well protected by horseshoes, a couple of which are old and venerable. The present owners, fascinated with tales of witchery, have also added some of their own. The ruins of the seventeenth-century barn, where John Nutter's sick cow may have breathed her last, make a picturesque sight. It is more than likely that within the ruins lie buried other protective devices which have gone unnoticed.

Bulls are still very much in evidence at Bull Hole Farm. On a recent walk around the farmhouse and its surrounding fields, my son and I found our way ahead blocked by three magnificent males, who took time out from mating with a resigned and rather bored-looking cow to bellow a noisy warning. Not feeling particularly courageous, we decided to take a different path and leave the bulls to pester the cow in peace.

On the same visit we noticed a stone structure that upon investigation turned out to be a large well. This led us to wonder whether, perhaps, this could be a sacred spring associated with the speculative Norse temple site further down the hill. This particular well is called, aptly enough, 'Puck, or Rob's (Robin Goodfellow's) Well', and as I have pointed out, ancient pagan sites of worship often became associated with the fairies and other supernatural beings.[45] It is interesting to note that in a 1628 pamphlet, Robin Goodfellow's chief companion bears the name of Tibb! [46]

As if to emphasise the point, on approaching Puck's Well above Bull Hole, a large hare bounded out of the undergrowth and peered at myself and my son rather indignantly before powering off down the hill. We very much hoped it was indeed Mother Demdike's familiar spirit Tibb, and shouted an enthusiastic greeting as it disappeared.

In the absence of a horseshoe, anything manufactured out of iron could be employed as a witch or fairy repellent. Knives and scissors were buried under the doorstep or placed beneath the doormat so that a witch could not gain entry to the house. Butter churns could be protected by a knife placed beneath, and in the event of the butter not 'coming', a hot iron or poker was inserted into the cream to drive out the witch. Iron implements could also be suspended in the shippen to protect the animals.[47] Robert Herrick comments in verse:

> Hang up the hook and shears to scare
> Hence the hag that rides the mare,
> Till they be all over wet
> With the mire and the sweat:
> This observ'd, the manes shall be
> Of your horses all knot free.[48]

While objects made of iron represented a major deterrent, there were other substances traditionally believed to possess valuable, intrinsic anti-witch properties. Rowan wood, along with various objects made of stone, and even old shoes could all be deployed as weapons in the constant battle against the dark powers of the evil witch and her familiar.

CHAPTER THREE

Witchwood, Witchstones and Old Shoes

Oh Master, oh Master, we can't do no good
She's got a witch cross made o' mountain ash wood.[1]

 sk Lancashire folk these days the best way to protect yourself against a witch and they are most likely to tell you to get yourself a piece of rowan wood. While many of the old remedies have been forgotten over the years, folk memory of this tree's efficacy in averting evil lingers on. The rowan has been a holy tree for thousands of years. Druids were said to wreath the heads of their sacrificial bulls with the wood and light bonfires of rowan before battle. Brigantia, our local Celtic goddess, used rowan-wood arrows and in Norse mythology the tree was sacred to Thor, who was saved from drowning in a raging torrent when one of the trees bent its branches over and pulled him out of the water.

The Sacred Tree

The rowan has several alternative names, including mountain ash, wiggen and the witch tree. A mysterious tree by any reckoning (its very name meaning 'secret lore' in Old Norse), its berries form the magical sign of the pentagram, or five-pointed star, where they join the stalk. Some consider these fruits to be the preferred food of the *Tuatha De Danaan*. These beings were old gods from Irish mythology that were later regarded as fairies. It has been suggested that if you were unfortunate or stupid enough to damage a rowan then the fay would exact revenge by making you extremely ill.

Other sources, however, maintain that rowan was actively disliked by many (presumably malicious) fairies and practically everyone agrees that witches positively detested it. Bearing in mind the suggested partnership between the witch and her fairy familiar, it will come as no surprise that the tree was used to protect against the *maleficia* of both witch and fairy. Necklaces of rowan berries were, for example, hung around the necks of children to make sure they were not kidnapped by fairies, and were also worn to protect victims from the evil eye of witches. The red hue of the berries was considered to be the most potent of all the colours for defensive purposes.

It was thought that in order to be fully effective, a branch of rowan must be severed with a domestic knife and cut on St Helen's Day from a tree that was completely unknown to the cutter. Having found the tree in this random manner it was necessary to return home by a completely different route. So powerful was the protection afforded by the rowan that its wood was utilised to make all types of domestic and farm implements, including handles for ploughs, pitchforks and shovels. It was even used to fashion a particular architectural element incorporated into the fabric of certain houses. This feature acted as a permanent charm against witchcraft and was known as a witch post.

Witch Posts

A witch post is generally found in extremely old cruck houses of timber-framed construction. It forms the end post by the side of the fireplace, which in turn supports the beam across the front of the hearth.[2] Usually (but not always) it would have protective symbols carved upon it, as well as varying numbers of horizontal bands and occasionally a date. One of the best examples, found in Scarborough in Yorkshire (now in the Pitt Rivers collection in Oxford), is decorated with several interesting patterns. These include a St Andrew's cross upon the arms of which are carved hearts pricked with pins, representations of different phases of the moon and what look like horseshoes – all familiar designs in the world of *apotropaia*.[3] The symbol of the heart (representing life force) is an oft-used one in protective decoration and was used on anything from jewellery designed to protect children[4] to everyday items like apple corers.[5]

The choice of a St Andrew's cross (also known as a saltire cross) was probably quite deliberate. Any cross is an ancient cosmic axis symbol signifying order.[6]

It would also, of course, have provided Christian protection. The saltire cross, however, may have been chosen specifically because the origin of this form is derived from an old French and Old English word meaning 'a cross-shaped barrier', or barricade (from *saulter*, to jump). Humans could jump over this barrier, but animals could not. Probably, then, this form of the symbol was used as a permanent barrier against creatures perceived to be not entirely human. This would apply to witches in their spirit guise as well as the fairy folk.

The actual positioning of the witch post in the house was all-important. It was always placed so that it could protect the hearth area, an easy point of access for a witch or her familiar. Such features are comparatively rare. Most witch posts seem to be located in North Yorkshire and until comparatively recently, only one example has been noted in Lancashire. Located in an old cottage called New Houses (Numbers 3–5), on Newchurch Road in Newchurch-in-Rossendale, this particular post was inspected and drawn by a Mr James Walton in 1959.[7] It protects a door and fireplace in what is evidently the classic position and is adorned by the usual saltire cross along with two horizontal bars and four vertical 'peg' or 'person' shapes beneath.[8] It also appears that one of the owners of the cottage removed a human face from the post at some point in its history.[9] Human faces and heads were, as we will see, regarded as powerful anti-witch devices. We are fortunate that this Lancashire example is one of the very few to bear a date – in this case 1695. The post also bears the initials I. A., which is thought to stand for John Ashworth.[10]

The owner of the property in the 1960s had some very strange ideas about the purpose of his witch post. Mr Beard told a reporter for the *Rossendale Free Press* in 1967 that it was called a 'Devil's Cross', and that witches were tied to the post and tried for witchcraft in his house.[11] Needless to say this complete misunderstanding of the function of the witch post resulted in some later owners of the property finding it difficult to obtain willing babysitters! Other witch posts have been identified at Higher Constable Lee, just outside Rawtenstall, while a third was discovered fairly recently in the same neighbourhood. Another is rumoured to exist in Bass House, Gollinrod, near Summerseat.

Lancastrians lacking the advantage of a witch post in their houses defended the hearth and chimney in various other ways. Being the heart and soul of the home, the hearth had to be guarded vigilantly. This area of the house was always considered particularly vulnerable as it was an easy point of entry for a malignant entity, be it witch spirit or fairy. It was also one of the dirtiest and blackest parts

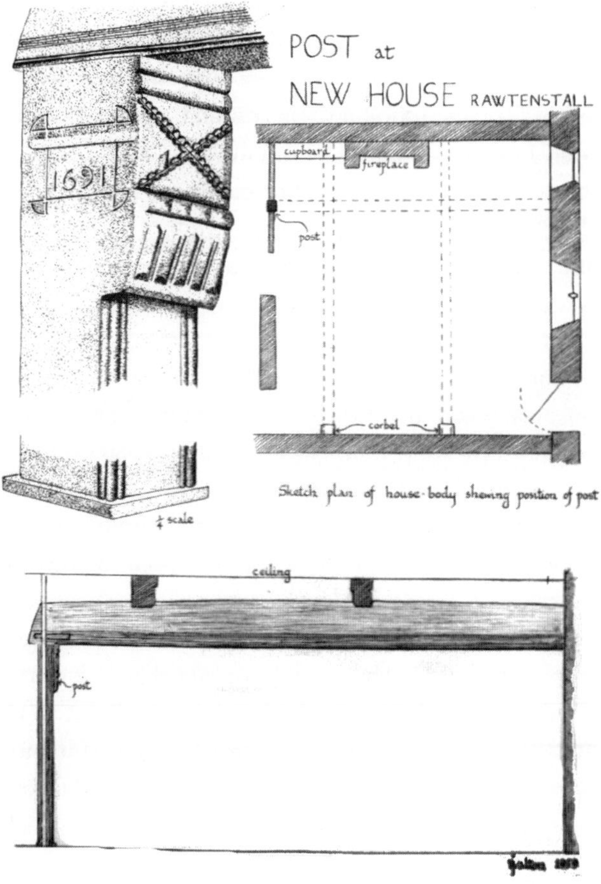

POST at
NEW HOUSE RAWTENSTALL

1691

Drawing of witch post in New Houses cottage c. 1959

Sketch plan of house·body shewing position of post

⅓ scale

cupboard

fireplace

post

corbel

ceiling

post

of the house and as such was considered particularly attractive to evil spirits of all kinds. Housewives would decorate the hearth stone with whorls and maze patterns, to protect the chimney from these persistent supernatural pests.[12] The historian Clifford Byrne says that when his mother was a young girl she saw a large hearthstone in a farm on Pendle decorated in this manner. 'A line marked by blue limestone was started in the ashes of the fire, which came into the hearthstone, then worked its way across the stone in whorls, round and round and round, until it reached the other side, when it was again taken into the ashes.'[13]

These patterns were thought to confuse both witch and fairy, holding them up while they wandered around getting themselves lost within the design. Some fairy lore enthusiasts consider that the fay folk only like to travel in straight lines, though why this should be I cannot imagine.

Protection against *maleficia* could even be extended to the fire irons. On display at Clitheroe Castle Museum, for example, is a splendid poker decorated with a cross of St Andrew. However, the most common way Lancastrians and indeed folk all over the country protected their hearth, chimney and other points of access was by the curious custom of walling up an old shoe.

Concealed Shoes and Boots

Reports of old shoes coming to light during building renovations are becoming more and more common as their significance has slowly come to be recognised. The Museum of Leathercraft in Northampton receives on average a report of one such discovery per month, and these finds can now be counted in thousands rather than hundreds. Most of the recorded shoes date from between the fourteenth and twentieth centuries and are often old, used and rather revolting specimens. Sometimes footwear has been concealed with associated objects, including other items of dress, clay pipes, glass artefacts and even dried chickens![14]

The majority of the finds have been discovered in the chimney or hearth area, an example of which (a child's boot dating from the 1880s) came to light some years ago stuffed up a chimney at the Talbot Head Hotel, Strawclough near Rochdale. Other popular spots for finding shoes include the roof and under floorboards. On display at Clitheroe Castle Museum is a tiny child's shoe, which was found under floorboards at the top of the attic stairs of a late seventeenth-century house in the village of Yealand Conyers, near Lancaster. This was associated with five glass bottles and an unidentified artefact made of leather and rope. Rebecca Shawcross, the Shoe Resources Officer at Northampton Museum, commented, ' ... What a delightful little shoe it is ... It is a latchet tie shoe with what looks like a very low heel, though the images are a little dark for me to be 100%. It is early and so all hand sewn. I would say from the style of fastening, toe shape [and] general look that it dates to the seventeenth century – 1660s–1670s. It would certainly fit in with the date of the house.' [15] Another very fine example of a pair of children's shoes dating from about 1800 was discovered under floorboards during building work at The Aspinall Arms at Mitton, near Clitheroe, in 2007.

The precise motivation behind the custom is a subject of continuing academic debate. Some archaeologists think that hidden shoes are associated with fertility and cite as support the rhyme of the old woman who lived in a shoe that was overrun with children. Also, shoes are traditionally tied to the car of the newly married.

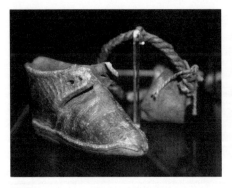 

Child's shoe, c. 1660
from Yealand Conyers
(Clitheroe Castle Museum)

Pair of children's shoes c. 1800,
discovered under floorboards in the
Aspinall Arms, Mitton

Most researchers of *apotropaia*, however, incline towards the view that concealing shoes seems to be a largely male superstition – one that was in some way intended to protect the house from witches, nasty fairies and evil spirits of every description. People may have thought that an old, worn shoe had soaked up the 'essence' of the wearer, and so personified the owner whose own spirit would therefore stand guard against evil. A shoe might also have been regarded as an effective 'evil spirit trap'. In *The Archaeology of Ritual and Magic*, Ralph Merrifield draws attention to the legend of an unofficial Buckinghamshire saint, John Schorn, who was said to have conjured the Devil into a boot.[16] Whatever virtue the shoe or boot possessed, it seemed that even a drawing of a shoe could have some protective potential. Some crude outlines of footwear have been found scratched on lead roofs of churches, and an interesting example is on display in the Shire Hall at Lancaster Castle.

George Wolfenden of Fooden Cottage, in Bolton-by-Bowland, near Clitheroe, unearthed an interesting find in his late seventeenth-century home. During building work, he came across a small inglenook fireplace that had been bricked up and plastered over, behind which had been concealed about a dozen pairs of children's clogs. Mr Wolfenden took these to Ribchester Museum for an opinion and was told that the custom harked back to pagan human sacrifice. Rather than sacrificing actual children as a ritual to protect a new building, he was told that their shoes were substituted instead.[17] This, then, is yet another potential (if a little sinister) explanation for this strange custom.

Mr Wolfenden replaced the little clogs behind a skirting board, where maybe he hoped they would continue to protect the building. There have been several reports of hauntings that have commenced after concealed shoes were removed, so many residents that find such artefacts are anxious to return the shoe charm to its original position once it has been examined and photographed.[19] Failing to do so, they believe, would result in a haunting or general bad luck. Alternatively, some people place the shoes in a prominently positioned display case where they can be admired by all but at the same time continue to protect the building.

While rowan often proved itself as a most effective and powerful deterrent against witches, and shoes were designed to trap frolicking familiars before they could do any harm, in a county famed far and wide for its plentiful and troublesome witches, Lancastrians had to make sure they had plenty more tricks up their sleeves. When it came to protecting their property from hags intent on doing them a mischief, one of the most important weapons in the armoury was harnessed in the shape of stone objects. In order to be able to understand the power attributed to stone in all its different guises we need to understand that in times past, stones were worshipped as living things capable of performing tasks such as healing and protecting property.

Children's shoe c. 1660 and associated objects found at Yealand Conyers
(Clitheroe Castle Museum)

The Enchanted Stones

Archaeologists are sometimes puzzled at how frequently white pebbles (usually, but not always, made of quartz) turn up in a ritual context. The sanctity of such stones certainly traces its origin as far back as biblical times. The Book of Revelation tells us that 'To him that overcometh will I give to eat of the hidden manna, and will give him a white stone, and in the stone a new name written, which no man knoweth saving he that receiveth it.' [20]

In the *Leech Book of Bald* (a herbal probably compiled in Winchester in about 920 AD) we are given the Anglo-Saxon take on the use of the white stone: 'The white stone is powerful against stitch, and against flying venom, and against all unknown maladies.' At this time, the pain known as 'the stitch' and many other illnesses were thought to be caused by elf shot. These were sharp, poisonous little flint arrows that the elf or witch loved to fire unexpectedly at any passing animal or human. Infection was known as 'flying venom' and the 'unknown' maladies were mysterious because they were thought to be caused by witchcraft. Should someone be fortunate enough to find an 'elf bolt', or possess a 'lucky' white stone, then it could be immersed in water which was then drunk to protect against bad luck, ill-health and witchcraft. [21]

The idea of a special stone being submerged in water and used for healing both natural and unnatural illnesses persisted through the centuries and was still very current in seventeenth-century thinking, when Lancashire wise-folk would often use such healing aids. Water that had been in contact with stone is sometimes also met within other contexts. Just off Trapp Lane at Simonstone, near Read, is a wart well in the form of a natural boulder inscribed with the words 'Simon's Cross', together with a cross symbol. This was perhaps used originally as a stone (or hoarstone) that marked the boundary between Read and Simonstone and once served as the base for a wayside cross, long disappeared. The rainwater that collects in the empty socket seems to be infused with certain minerals and has for many years been known as an effective wart cure. Whether the wart well boulder is the stone referred to in the name Simonstone is not clear.

Another example of the use of protective stone is the placing of 'thunderstones' (in reality Neolithic stone axes) in the roofs and walls of buildings. It was thought that when lightning struck the ground, the thunderstone would be its physical manifestation and would therefore protect the house from lightning as well as *maleficia*. A good example of a thunderstone was apparently found by Jack and Brenda Sagar, enclosed in the wall of a cottage they were renovating at Sabden Fold, near Newchurch-in-Pendle. [22]

Hagstones

Stone, then, was regarded as a magical, sacred substance and as such could be used both to heal mysterious illness and deflect *maleficia* in general. A particularly revered and effective type of defensive stone came in the form of a pebble with a natural hole in it, known in Lancashire as a hagstone. The many names given to these holed stones are a testament to their importance and use over a wide geographical area. These alternative names include witchstones, fairystones, eyestones, dobbie stones, wishstones, nightmare stones and occasionally Ephialtes stones (the latter meaning 'he who jumps upon', the name of a Greek dæmon of nightmare rather than the betrayer of the 300 Spartans).

Hagstones were hung in barns and shippens to prevent witches from riding cattle and horses during the dark hours of night. The earliest reference to the use of such stones in this way dates from the first half of the fifteenth century. Margaret Pearson, the Padiham witch tried alongside the Pendle witches in 1612, was accused of hag riding by her fellow witch, Mother Chattox, who said of her, ' ... the wife of one Pearson of Paddiham is a very euill woman ... and that she ... hath done very much harme to one Dodgesons goods, who came in at a loop-hole into the said Dodgesons Stable, and shee and her spirit together did sit upon his Horse or Mare, until the said Horse or Mare died.' [23]

Margaret, then, had managed to get into the stable through a hole in the wood, and she and her familiar spirit (a man with cloven feet) had a fine old time sitting heavily upon the poor horse's back until it died. Mr Dodgson had evidently been very remiss and had not protected his stable with a holed stone. Most farmers maintained that a witch could not get in once a hagstone had been placed in the stable. Hopefully, after the antics of Margaret Pearson and her spirit, Mrs Dodgson bought her husband a nice hagstone for Christmas!

Curiously, sheep are seldom mentioned in relation to hagstones or indeed any other sort of traditional protection against witchcraft. J. Geoffrey Dent proposes that the reason for this probably lies in the relative unimportance of sheep to the small-scale farmer and cottager. He makes the point that large tracts of land are required for sheep rearing, so while the ordinary villager therefore played very little part in sheep farming, his cow was of a personal possession and had to be defended at all costs. Examples of sheep protection charms are therefore few and far between.

Humans were also able to benefit from the stone's protection by enjoying nightmare-free sleep if they hung a holed stone above their bed head. Nightmares were believed to be caused by a hag, or witch, sitting heavily on the stomach during sleep. This was often as a result of a state of consciousness in which the

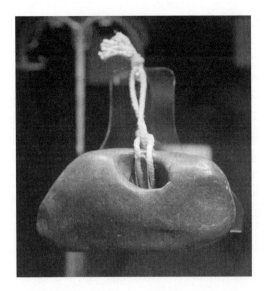

Example of a hagstone
(Clitheroe Castle Museum)

sleeper thought he was awake but felt as if he was being held down unable to move. (These days, victims of this condition are more likely to blame it on unwanted attention from extra-terrestrials!)

According to an anonymous and undated account of the history of Chatburn (near Clitheroe), several hagstones of various shapes and sizes and containing strings were discovered when the old smithy was demolished in Chatburn village.[24] This may be the same smithy mentioned in the Court rolls of Clitheroe in 1662, located 'at the east bridge of Chattburne', at that time rented by John Dobson for 6d per year.[25]

Chatburn does not figure in the trials of the Lancashire witches, yet curiously the village has proved to be something of a happy hunting ground for anti-witch-craft charms. One of these artefacts was, as far as I am aware, a unique example of its type and it is therefore extremely regrettable to report its recent destruction. This charm was located in a row of cottages called Beech Grove and took the form of a crude plaster face of a male. It was fashioned upon a piece of projecting stone in the loft of the end cottage, and introduces us to the extremely interesting phenomena of protective and evil-averting stone heads. Few witches could escape the watchful eye of the Celtic heads that protected many properties in Pendle and further afield. J. B. Taylor has come up with a clever analogy for the way in which protective heads were thought to function: 'The modern day equivalent is television surveillance as used in some shops, factories, motorways and posh houses.'[26]

The Padiham witch Margaret Pearson and her demon familiar hag-riding Dodgeson's mare (drawing by Annabel Spenceley)

The Lost Guardian of Beech Grove

This important plaster head first came to my attention in 1989 when I was assisting Dr Ralph Merrifield – the late Deputy Director of the Museum of London and author of *The Archaeology of Ritual and Magic* – with his research into domestic ritual charms. The owners of the eighteenth-century cottage at Beech Grove were eager to introduce me to their friend in the loft, and took immense pleasure in regaling me with stories about how all the electrics in the property went haywire when they discovered him, and subsequently had him photographed by the local paper. Having later bought a property in the same row of houses when I moved back to Lancashire from London in 2002, I can well believe this.

The Beech Grove electrical supply and many pieces of household equipment regularly played up when I lived there and at one point my clock decided to go backwards. On another occasion, at about nine o'clock at night on Christmas Eve, my son and I were commenting to each other that the evening was dragging. As if it had heard me, the clock's hands whizzed forwards in time about three hours in a few seconds. Relieved, we decided the evening could officially be declared at an end and took ourselves off to bed.

And don't get me started on the television, which developed a mind of its own and switched itself on and off with gay abandon. All this curious activity may have been due to the quarrying which has taken place for many years near the site of the house, or possibly to underground streams which run beneath the property. All I know is that life at Beech Grove could be very exciting at times, although I suspect that former residents may have found some of the goings-on alarming, which may go some way to explaining the presence of multiple paranormal protection in this particular row of houses!

The owners of the Beech Grove plaster head informed me that neighbours had superstitiously advised them to get rid of the feature. Luckily, however, those particular people were sensitive to the history of their property and believed that it was an historical curiosity well worth preserving. They also felt that he was looking after their house, which would indeed seem to have been his primary intended function. The head, 43 cm high and 29 cm wide, was positioned on a stone on the gable-end wall so that it could gaze right across the lofts of the other properties in the row.

Having wobbled about on a step ladder taking photos of the plaster head, these were duly sent off to Dr Merrifield who commented on their receipt, 'I'm sure you're right about the Chatburn head being protective. I hope you didn't

Plaster head at Beech Grove, Chatburn

upset the electrical arrangements again with your photography! The stone outside looks remarkably like a medieval corbel re-used and they do of course often have human heads on them. Is there —or was there – a substantial medieval stone building, such as a ruined abbey, from which the corbel might have been removed, anywhere in the neighbourhood?' [27]

I was able to inform Ralph that we were actually spoilt for choice as far as ruined abbeys went, having those of Sawley and Whalley close by. However, I felt it more likely that any re-used stone masonry was just as likely to have come from the ruined chapel of St Martin in Chatburn itself. This building once lay close by, only a field's distance from the property in question and was still in existence in the seventeenth century.

Dr Merrifield considered the Chatburn head to be an extremely important and significant example of a human face, intentionally fashioned to protect the whole row of properties from all manner of ills including witchcraft and evil spirits. Information concerning its discovery was forwarded to Manchester Museum, to enable its details to be included in their research into Celtic stone heads in the North West. In a letter to Dr Merrifield, M. N. Petch commented:

Plaster heads are rare in comparison to those of stone and this is a fascinating example. I would agree wholeheartedly with your belief that the head is not of great antiquity, nevertheless it was without doubt apotropaic, evil-averting or luck bringing and therefore fits within the general scheme of the Celtic Head cult. You are right to point out a comparison with the Rochdale head. Clearly it is bearded. It conveys an almost waterworn appearance and reminds me of the wizard's face at the Wizard's well at Alderley Edge in Cheshire ... it has that same eerie expressionless gaze that most Celtic heads reproduce.[28]

Apotropaic stone heads seem to proliferate in the Pendle and Ribble Valley areas, no doubt as a response to both the trials of 1612, and any subsequent witchcraft cases in the area. Manchester Museum has catalogued many of these heads, and John Billingsley in his 'Stony Gaze', has carried out a meticulous and exhaustive investigation into Celtic and other stone heads (for which he has coined the term 'archaic' heads) in the Calder Valley and West Yorkshire.[29] The reader is referred to this excellent study should they wish to explore the background of the Celtic head cult in more depth. Suffice it to say here that in the Iron Age, human severed heads were considered an extremely powerful talisman and were used to adorn temples, sacred wells and tribal homesteads.

The head was considered to contain the very essence of a person to whom it belonged to such an extent that even a representation of a severed head became an object of extreme magical power.[30] This *apotropaic* authority attributed to the severed head motif has continued to hold sway to within living memory in the Pendle and Ribble Valley districts.

The Watcher on the Threshold

Stone heads were often chosen, therefore, to keep a watchful eye on the entrances to many buildings in the neighbourhood infested by the Lancashire witches. Once thought to be genuinely ancient examples of Iron Age art, many have now been assigned a far more recent date. Examples occur that seem to date from medieval times, while others are dated as late as the nineteenth century. Occasionally, what appears to be a genuine Iron Age head will turn up. The Rochdale head mentioned by Manchester Museum that now greets visitors to the Touchstones Visitors Centre in Rochdale, may be a genuinely ancient example. The larger head alongside it is considered to be of a much more recent date.

Ralph Merrifield commented about the archaic heads discovered in Pendle and the Ribble Valley:

Is it possible, I wonder, that we are dealing with a local 'folk art' that grew up to remedy a deficiency when the supply of medieval sculpture from abbeys etc. ran out? It seems to me possible, if belief in their prophylactic powers had become firmly established. It would account for the varying degrees of skill and artistic quality as well as the varied prototypes ... I don't know of any that are quite certainly ancient except the stone head from Caerwent, but I suspect the tradition did begin with the Celtic head-cult, so the possibility that some of the Lancashire heads are ancient can't be ruled out.[31]

The majority of these heads have certain features in common. They usually demonstrate 'flat' features with a triangular nose and oval, bulging eyes. One of the most curious features of many stone heads is a slit or cigarette hole in the vicinity of the mouth. Some think such heads may represent Celtic gods and that the holes might have been used for some ritual purpose such as giving drinks to the god during ceremonies, or perhaps for holding a pipe or branch. In *Stony Gaze*, however, John Billingsley suggests the more mundane explanation that the heads may have been set up as target practice in a similar fashion to an Aunt Sally fair stall. A pipe would be put in the hole drilled for the purpose, and objects thrown at it to try to dislodge the pipe from the mouth. As he says, this may explain the extremely battered state of many of the archaic heads he has studied.[32]

A stone head noticed by Ms. Smith in her pamphlet on stone heads,[33] which is located at Moor Game Hall Farm, Dutton, has been painted by children and has, she said, been used as a shooting target. This example certainly seems to offer some support for Mr Billingsley's theory. However, while it may explain away some of the holes in the mouths of archaic stone heads, I find it a little improbable that it can provide the explanation for all of them, implying as it does a total lack of respect for these objects. The jury is still out on this one.

As well as guarding entrances, stone heads can be found in field walls and enclosed deliberately within the fabric of house walls. They seem to guard 'liminal' or threshold areas, where the veil between this world and the world of the supernatural was thought to be particularly thin, thus rendering these areas vulnerable to attack by 'the other'. Some examples have, for whatever reason, been buried in what appears to be open ground. These may be offerings of some sort, or may have been buried in fear, to 'kill' the supernatural object. Alternatively, the intention may have been to assist the fertility of the soil or even to cure land blasted by witchcraft.

Whatever their date, it certainly appears to be a tradition in Witch Country for householders to protect their threshold by placing a stone head on guard. As well as guarding homesteads, heads were also placed above barn doors to protect the animals from any passing witch or demon. A good example of a protective stone head such as this can be found at Dinkling Green Farm out in the wilds of the Trough of Bowland. As the farm is owned by the Duchy of Lancaster, I was jokingly (I hope) informed that I would need Her Majesty's permission to view the stone head, which is placed on a pedestal above a shippen door. Carved out of sandstone, the face has two 'cigarette holes' in its mouth and is about 10 inches high. This may be a rare example of a genuinely ancient Celtic head, used to provide a guard for the cattle in this remote spot in Bowland.

One of my personal favourites of all the stone heads in the area has to be 'George', a head carved out of granite, about one foot high, which was originally discovered when numbers 15 and 16 Church Lane, Whalley, were knocked into one property. It was walled up between these two eighteenth-century properties and later moved with the owner to neighbouring Poole End in The Square, where it was inherited by Dorothy and David Winstanley. Bearing in mind that Whalley Abbey lies within yards of these properties, it is quite likely that George is an example of a 'grotesque' medieval carving removed from the abbey ruins and walled up to act as an unseen guardian of the houses.

The abbey was often plundered for its stone. In 1990 a member of the Lancaster Archaeological Unit (excavating at the abbey) mentioned to me in conversation that a 90-year-old lady had been regaling the archaeologists with tales of how, when she was young, she and her friends had pinched several gargoyles from the abbey to decorate their houses! Other grotesques can be found on a property at nearby Painter Wood in Billington, just outside Whalley, and these also probably represent plunder from the abbey.

Mike Yates, a record producer of Berwick on Tweed, made this comment about George, and I hope he will not mind if I quote what he says in full because he puts forward an interesting theory about the role played by some stone heads:

Some years ago a friend of mine was knocking a hole through an interior wall of her house. This was in the Lancashire village of Whalley, and in the rubble she found a life-size stone carving of a human head. Experts were called and she was told that this was similar to a number of other heads found inside ancient walls. Most, apparently had been found in Lancashire and Yorkshire. I tell this story because Bert Lloyd once told me of a Balkan ballad about a young girl who is 'walled up' and left to die in a new building. In Bulgaria it is known as Trima bratya dyulgeri (The Walled-in Bride) ... And I just wonder if, at one time, blood had to be spilt when a

'George' enjoying a cigarette, and below, in his special niche in the bar

new building was being erected. Were the stone heads representative of a tradition in which human sacrifice was once a necessary part of the building process ... ?[34]

Mr Yates may be right that George was used in lieu of a building sacrifice (much like the children's clogs at Bolton-by-Bowland), though personally I find it more likely that both sets of artefacts were placed in the wall to watch out for witches and their evil spirits. George was possibly intended to fulfil both functions.

Originally adorning the fireplace of his new home in Poole End, George now resides in a special niche in a bar in the living room. Looking extremely self-satisfied and grinning at everyone, he happily presides over the serving of alcoholic spirits (while still no doubt keeping a wary eye out for spirits of the evil variety). As George has the usual 'cigarette hole' in his mouth, he is sometimes given a cigarette to puff on for a bit of enjoyment. He has this in common with another stone head found during building work at Straits, Easton, in Dorset. This example was also found in a wall, this time embedded in the wall rubble of the scullery of a seventeenth-century cottage. 'The effigy, an ugly fellow with empty eye sockets, a squat nose and a little round hole of a mouth into which the workmen stuck a cigarette to lighten his gruesome appearance, will remain exposed to become part of the decor of the room.'[35]

Also protecting a house, but this time placed in an exterior position, are archaic heads which gaze down on anyone or anything about to enter the porch of Bank Hall in Barrowford. Now known as The Lamb Club, the building dates from 1696 and is located on Church Street. This particular example is known as a panel head and Ms. Green quotes from a book published by The Friends of Park Hall 'Bank Hall is a building rich in vernacular character ... Take a look at the kneelers on the cross wing which have carved faces on them, that on the left looking down on the porch! These are reminders that in the 1690s fear of witch-craft still lingered in Pendle and charms were thought worth trying.' [36]

The final stone head we will look at is well worth the wait and again has real and tangible connections with the witches of Pendle and most specifically, with Mother Demdike.

The Wizard of the Stonepit

Within sight of Bull Hole Farm, just off Well Head Road near Newchurch, is a disused quarry known as Faugh's. In the quarry, carved upon a large rock, is a superb bearded archaic head that watches solemnly and steadily over the place.

The carved head at Faugh's quarry

Traditionally, the quarry is the site of the 'Stonepit in Gouldshey' where Mother Demdike first met her familiar spirit Tibb in about 1592.[37] It was also in this location that Tibb first asked Demdike for her soul in return for anything she wanted, and here she agreed to the bargain. It has been recorded that this stone head, known locally as 'the wizard of the stonepit', was carved to pay tribute to the memory of a quarry worker who died there. However, this type of story about the presence of stone heads is a very common one indeed, and often seems to be told in an attempt to rationalise the existence of an artefact that had a more occult and superstitious significance.

As the traditional place[38] where an evil spirit accosted one of the most famous witches in history, this must have seemed a potentially very haunted and dangerous spot to the local people. It is not surprising, therefore, that a stone head should have been carved in the stonepit to act as an eternal guardian. Those gazing, watchful eyes continue to keep a sharp look out for another Tibb, and would hopefully scare him away before he could lead any more passing witches into temptation (annoying, of course, if you happen to go there with the specific intention of communing with an evil spirit or two!).

The church authorities of Newchurch-in-Pendle, the village that features so often in the story of the Lancashire witches of 1612, made absolutely certain that no evil spirits or witches were able creep surreptitiously around St Mary's Church with nefarious intentions. For the church tower boasts the famous 'all-seeing eye of God' that ensures any witches and demons entering the churchyard will have a beady eye kept upon their activities at all times.[39] This is an interesting way to reassure the people of the village, reducing as it does the idea of a stone head guardian to its essential essence – the ever-watchful eye which sees all and protects against any supernatural predator.

Witchstones

As mentioned earlier, the village of Chatburn, near Clitheroe, is something of a happy hunting ground for the student of *apotropaia*. Situated again at Beech Grove is a very worn example of another type of stone anti-witch charm. High up on the wall of a property that was once the coach house is a stone upon which the faint outline of a horned animal can just about be identified. This is what is known as a witchstone – used to protect cattle from *maleficia* – and is very similar indeed to another very fine example which turned up at the Red Pump Inn at Bashall Eaves in about 1990.

Originally found in rubble at the back of the pub near an old barn, the Red Pump witchstone (carved in sandstone) has had a very chequered career. The tenant of the public house, Jim Fenton, said in the *Clitheroe Advertiser and Times* in 1990, 'It doesn't look like a normal gargoyle to me and it looks like a ram's head, which made me wonder if it was something to do with the occult. After all, we can see Pendle clearly from here … ' According to the newspaper, 'Between the barleycorn-like braided hair and the face of the ram is what looks like a witch's broomstick.'

In response to the article, a Mr L. Grant-Townsend of Clitheroe identified the artefact as a witchstone, having seen similar examples protecting barns when he was living near Settle. One, he said, bore a goat's head similar to the Red Pump's, while another had the rough facial outline of a monk or nun (actually more like an archaic head) and the third bore a circle. As he commented, 'In such a district as this with its rich legend, witch history and folklore, it is not surprising that, in the course of building renovations, carved stones of this nature are found.'

Needless to say the publicity resulting from the discovery of the witchstone stimulated claims of supposed spectral activity. Mr Fenton commented to the *Clitheroe Advertiser and Times*, 'When we first moved in here over two years ago, we did hear strange noises, like people going in and out of the building.' None of Mr Fenton's family liked the look of the stone, and neither did my former next door neighbour, Debbie Wadsworth of Beech Grove, who happened to be working in the pub at that time. She described how she became very perturbed and yelled, 'Get that thing OUT of here!', when she first saw it. According to tradition, only a witch could possibly take such strong exception to a witchstone, and I very much wanted to poke her with a horseshoe or wave a hagstone at her to test her reaction, but with difficulty I managed to refrain from doing so!

Having travelled up from London to examine and photograph this important artefact in early 1990, I thought it well worthwhile reporting this latest find to

St Mary's Church, Newchurch-in-Pendle

The famous 'all-seeing eye'

The Red Pump Witchstone in its new home at Great Mitton Hall

Dr Merrifield. He found the stone fascinating and made the following comment, 'My first impression of the stone from the Red Pump was that it was a rather bizarre version of the classical *bucranium* ornament and probably seventeenth or eighteenth century. The 'witches' brooms' are simply tassels and the stone itself might have been part of the frieze of a rather splendid classical style building, in which the skulls (normally ox skulls) would alternate with festoons of flowers, fruit, etc., as in the Temple of Vesta at Tivoli. I am pretty sure it is derived from such a Roman architectural ornament, made more skull-like to appeal to some perverse local taste. If there are similar stones about in the same area, it would be likely that they came from the same frieze.' [40]

He went on to say that he certainly considered the stone to be a protective device against witchcraft, as there seemed very little reason otherwise to incorporate it in a building. The stone, he said, had certainly not been purpose made, as it was far too well carved, and must have come from the demolition of a very fine building. This 'very fine building' has never, unfortunately, been identified.

The *bucranium* (Latin for 'ox skull') decoration mentioned by Ralph was a classical motif that often featured on altars and was used in post-Roman buildings to emphasize their Roman 'style'. It is considered to be a reference to the garlanding of bulls before they were sacrificed and the practice of decorating the temple walls with skulls of the sacrificial animals. *Bucrania* were possibly employed as witchstones unconsciously as a substitute for the sacrifice of one of the owner's actual animals, in a bid to gain supernatural protection for the building which sheltered his stock. As Ralph comments in *The Archaeology of Ritual and Magic*, 'The use of part of an animal particularly the skull or jawbone, as a symbol of its sacrifice, was common in building deposits of Anglo-Saxon, mediaeval and later times.' [41] It is possible therefore, that the same motif was considered a powerful protective device.

A more mundane explanation of course might be that once upon a time, a farmer spotted some demolition debris and thought to himself, 'Eeh! There's one really creepy-looking stone – that'd be bound to scare away evil spirits. I'll put it on my barn to protect my animals!' He might then be emulated by another farmer who looked for a similar creepy stone to protect *his* barn, until eventually a tradition was created.

As a result of superstitious fear, the Red Pump witchstone was re-buried in the pub grounds but was subsequently dug up again by a later landlord and sold to a medical consultant. Clues to its present whereabouts offered by Debbie at Beech Grove and Sue Holden, the Community Heritage Manager at Clitheroe Library, at length led me to Great Mitton Hall in September 2010. Here I discovered that the stone had been built into the new extension of this beautiful medieval building which is thought to have briefly provided a home for John Webster, the author of *The Displaying of Supposed Witchcraft*, when he was acting as vicar of Mitton in 1649.[42] Now fulfilling its *apotropaic* function on behalf of humans rather than animals, the stone skull's eyes gaze at the front porch, checking out Mr and Mrs Kay's visitors. It was very reassuring indeed to learn that the stone had not, as I had feared, been wantonly destroyed.

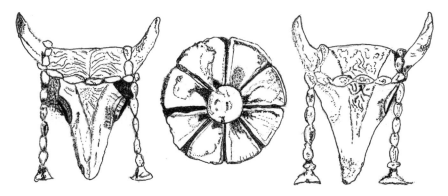

Garlanded bucrania, frieze ornament from temple complex at Samothrace, Greece
J.L.C.

Great Mitton Hall, the new home of the Red Pump witchstone

The traditional folk remedies involving witchstones, hagstones, stone heads, rowan wood in various shapes and forms, and old shoes, generally did the trick when familiar spirits were on the prowl and had to be stopped in their tracks. However, sometimes even these ancient, tried and tested measures failed to work against a really determined witch assault. If that was the case then you were really in trouble and in danger of losing the supernatural war against the legions of Satan. This was a scenario impossible to tolerate or even to contemplate, and demanded some very tough action indeed on the part of the beleaguered Lancastrian who saw a Lancashire witch skulking threateningly in every dark corner.

CHAPTER FOUR

White Witches, Written Charms and Witch Bottles

Welcome, welcome, happy be
In this blest Society.
Men and Beasts are in thy Power
Thou canst Save, and thou canstDevour
Thou canst Bless, and Curse the Earth
And cause Plenty, or a Dearth.[1]

he first line of defence – cold iron – had failed. The horseshoe hung up on the house and barn door had proved a waste of time, the shoe in the chimney had no effect whatsoever, and the hagstones had failed to prevent the horrid old crones from riding the horses ragged in the night. What was the bewitched, bothered and bewildered Lancastrian supposed to do next? The only alternative, and probably the last resort, was to pay someone to get rid of the witch and protect your family, home and animals against the potential onslaught of the hag and her vicious familiar spirits. Waiting in the wings was a set of people who set themselves up as experts in the occult by claiming that they could be relied upon to deal effectively with any number of pesky witches. From the seventeenth century and well into the nineteenth century, practically every village in Lancashire had its own individual, skilled in the ways of protective magic. It was time to call in the professional.

The Craft of the Wise

These occult practitioners were widely believed to be benevolent magicians that could be relied upon to sort out serious cases of evil witchery. They were variously known as wise-folk, cunning-folk, conjurers, wizards and white witches. Why

Title Page, 'The Displaying of
Supposed Witchcraft',
by John Webster

most malevolent 'black' witches tended to be women and the majority of benevolent 'white' witches seemed to be men (particularly in the nineteenth century)
is a loaded question unfortunately beyond the scope of this particular book. The
wise-folk, then, not only succoured the bewitched but provided a wide variety of
services besides for their customers.

These included selling horoscopes, tracing lost property, providing charms to
cure sick animals and people (especially those made ill as a result of supernatural
attack), preventing spoilt ale and selling love charms. The wise-man aroused
mixed feelings among those who bought his services. Many clients must have
reached the end of their tethers. With nowhere else to turn they were extremely
grateful for any help they could get and probably thought the fees charged to be
worth every penny. Others (very often from the more educated classes) were not
so impressed.

In 1677, Dr John Webster of Clitheroe made the point in *The Displaying of Supposed Witchcraft* that if a wise-man got something right once, then everybody heard about it. If he got it wrong a hundred times, however, that was very soon forgotten. 'For so it is here in this North Country with our Figure-flingers and pretended Conjurers, Piss-Prophets, and Water Witches, that if they hit once, it is cryed up and told everywhere; but if they erre a hundred times, it is soon buried in silence and oblivion, and one fool will not take warning at anothers being cheated and deceived.' [2] 'Figure flingers' were astrologers and 'piss prophets' were quack doctors that diagnosed illness by asking the patient to taste their own urine and describe its qualities. As a matter of interest, the term 'urine' only came into use in the fourteenth century. Earlier, the concept was described by the word 'piss' – now considered rude and vulgar. 'Water Witches' were people who dowsed to find water.

Some names of Lancastrian wise-folk who helped people living in terror of witchcraft and its associated sickness have come down to us in historical records. One of these practitioners was called in to help a victim of Isabel Robey, the witch of Windle (near St Helens) who was tried at Lancaster in 1612 at the same time as the witches from Pendle. Peter Chaddock's wife fell out with Isabel Robey, and as a result Peter himself began to suffer with a bad neck, which he put down to Isabel's retaliatory spells. He therefore called in the wise-man James the Glover, also of Windle. James managed to cure Peter (we are not told how), but then Peter developed a thirst which was impossible to quench. He sent again for the wise-man, and James the Glover told him to take hold of a drink and say the following charm while drinking: 'The Deuill and Witches are not able to preuale against GOD and his Word.' This apparently did the trick, for a while at least.[3] Strangely, during the trial procedure, another witness, Margaret Lyon, reported that Peter Chadwick had already decided that Isabel Robey was *not* a witch. Apparently this change of heart resulted from his consulting a different wise-man called Halseworths.[4] The judge completely ignored Chadwick's contradictory evidence and Isabel hanged alongside the witches from Pendle Forest.

Another Lancashire wise-man called Henry Baggilie was hauled before the courts in 1634 for curing the sick by using charms. He was examined on 26th May at Chadderton, just outside Oldham, by Edmund Assheton. Baggilie described to Assheton how he had learnt his trade from his father who had been taught a very effective charm by a Dutchman about twenty years earlier. This comprised certain words and prayers that would bless and help any sick people or cattle. The charm ran thus:

I tell thee thou forespoken toothe and tonge, hearte and hearte raithe, three things thee boote moste, the father sonne and holighuoste.[5]

Henry added the remarkable information that whenever he was called in to heal a person or animal, as he was reciting his charm, the illness seemed to transfer to himself from the afflicted party. (Another wise-woman and healer – Mary Shawe of Croft – also commented in 1630 that when she went to sit with a sick pig, she 'took on' its unpleasant symptoms as she was healing it.)[6] Strictly speaking, Henry and Mary would appear to have been 'charmers' rather than wise-folk.[7] From the limited evidence available they appear to have treated everyday illness of people and cattle rather than sickness attributable to witchcraft, and Henry at least did not charge for his help. He commented during his trial that he had only been paid in meal (animal feed), cheese or commodities and had never accepted silver or any other reward, but this plea of 'mitigating circumstances' evidently fell on deaf ears. Edmund Assheton merely wrote one ominous word at the foot of the examination record – 'Witchcrafte'.

Of course, the wise-folk and the charmers always trod a perilous path, forever running a very real risk of being accused of the malevolent witchcraft they claimed to fight against. In *A Discourse of the Damned Art of Witchcraft* (1610), William Perkins made his feelings abundantly clear when he said, 'by Witches we understand not those onely which kill and torment: but all Diviners, Charmers, Juglers, all Wizzards, commonly called wisemen and wisewomen; yea, whosoever doe any thing (knowing what they doe) which cannot be effected by nature or art; and in the same number we reckon good Witches which doe no hurt but good, which doe not spoile and destroy, but save and deliver.' [8] As far as he was concerned, it would seem that the only good witch was a dead witch. It seems very likely that Roger Nowell had a copy of Perkins' book in his library and may have been influenced by the author's opinions when investigating the witches of Pendle Forest.

Therefore, should the wise-folk put a foot wrong, there was always the risk of being accused of *maleficia* and satanic witchcraft themselves. We have seen how Mother Demdike attempted to cure one of John Nutter's sick cows at Bull Hole, only to be accused instead of bewitching it to death once her well-meaning intervention had failed. We might note that there is no mention of John Nutter offering to pay Mother Demdike for her services. Chattox, too, was evidently regarded as a wise-woman. The wife of John Moore asked her to mend some drink that had been bewitched. The spell she used ran thus:

Three Biters hast thou bitten,
The Hart, ill Eye, ill Tonge;
Three Bitter shall be thy Boote,
Father, Sonne, and Holy Ghost
A Gods name.
Five Pater-nosters, five avies,
And a Creede,
In worship of five wounds,
of our Lord.[9]

The charm worked and mended the drink, so Chattox was infuriated when Mrs Moore kept moaning and complaining at her and, as a result, she sent Fancie to kill one of the Moore family cows.[10] The story effectively illustrates the ambiguous role of the wise-woman/malevolent witch and how that perceived role could change in the wink of an eye. Another early wise-man that came to grief before the courts was Thomas Hope, a blacksmith by trade who came from Aspull. In 1638 he claimed that his powers derived from washing in some special waters in Rome.[11]

John Collier, the eccentric eighteenth-century 'father of Lancashire dialect' – also known as Tim Bobbin – seemed to dislike 'conjurers' intensely. Indeed he was so exasperated by one particular Rochdale wise-man called George Clegg (also known as 'the Prickshaw witch'), that he attempted to blow him up. Collier tricked the wise-man into sitting on a chair under which he had packed a pound of gunpowder. Above the chair was suspended a bucket of water, which was supposed to douse the flames when the gunpowder went off. Collier originally wanted a bucket full of 'well-mixed turds and piss' to land on the wise-man and put out the fire. However, the owner of the house took exception to this idea, as the trick was to be carried out in her bedroom. Luckily for the unfortunate wise-man (and, one suspects, for Collier also, who presumably did not wish to have murder on his conscience), the water did actually cascade onto the victim at the same time as the gunpowder exploded. The resulting fire was thus success-fully doused, but not before the poor wizard's chair had been blown into the air with him still sitting on it. This led to much huffing and puffing by Clegg, but his demands for recompense merely led to more ridicule at the hands (or rather the pen) of John Collier.[12]

A wise-man practising near Colne in the 1870s – known as Old Langsettle – would attempt to impress his potential clients by bringing out his collection of dusty old occult tomes and consulting his 'magic glass' for possible answers to his customers' requirements.[13] These old books were a valuable possession of the wise-man, particularly from the seventeenth century onwards, as they impressed clients and could also provide him with effective charms to use. The books owned by one Lancashire wise-man called Owd Rollison – who lived at Roe Green, Worsley, in the nineteenth century – are known to us. They include *The Three Books of Occult Philosophy* by Cornelius Agrippa (1651), *Tables for Calculating Nativities* by Zadkiel (1834) and *Christian Astrology* (1659) by William Lilly.[14]

An ever-popular and useful addition to the library of any wise-man was Reginald Scot's *The Discoverie of Witchcraft* (reprinted in 1665). In this book Scot described and illustrated dozens of charms, talismans, rituals and formulas used by magical practitioners, to demonstrate how fraudulent and silly he considered the whole subject to be. He could hardly have predicted that his book would end up being seized upon – by the very wise-folk he despised – to be used as a sourcebook for impressive-looking charms and formulas! Every wise-man and woman had to be able to design impressive charms as they were needed to fulfil one of primary functions of the job. This was to manufacture written charms to protect clients against a specific act of *maleficia*, or to protect their houses, persons and farm buildings and cattle from general witchcraft attack.[15] In the wake of the 1612 Pendle trials, the local wise-folk no doubt experienced a very satisfying boost to their businesses.

Written Anti-witchcraft Charms

In 1825 some workmen demolishing a shippen at West Bradford near Clitheroe discovered something curious. A small square piece of paper fluttered down from one of the beams and upon inspection the workmen saw weird and mysterious characters written on it. When opened up, the paper measured 7¼ inches by 6 inches and was covered with many strange symbols. It also featured a table or square made up of 36 smaller squares, each of which contained a magical character drawn in red ink.

Luckily, the workmen did not destroy the piece of paper on sight, which often seems to be the response to such items. Instead it seems to have found its way into the hands of one Jeremiah Garnett, a local mill owner who lived at a property called Roefield, in Clitheroe. Fortuitously, one of Garnett's relatives happened to be Reverend Richard Garnett, Keeper of Printed Books at the British Museum. Reverend Garnett used the museum's extensive collection of magical manuscripts and his own considerable skills as a cryptographer to decipher what turned out to be an excellent example of a protective magical charm.

He worked out that the table to the top left was a magic square, called 'The Table of the Sun'. The sum of every row of six small squares – whether counted vertically, horizontally or diagonally – adds up to 111, the sum total being 666. The latter number will be familiar to those who have seen the film *The Omen* as 'the number of the beast' in Revelation xiii, 18: 'Here is wisdom. Let him that hath understanding count the number of the beast: for it is the number of a man; and his number is six hundred three score and six' [i.e. 666]. This was a favourite number in magical formulas and incantations and we need not imagine the charm's creator was attempting to summon the Anti-Christ!

To the right of the magic square are five magical characters. The one on the top left comprises symbols of the sun and the word written underneath is *machen*, which is the cabalistic name of the 'third heaven' over which the Archangel Michael reigns. Underneath the symbols of the sun lies the Archangel's symbol (looking like a number 4 ending in what looks like N) and his name.

Moving across, the next character at the centre top represents the Intelligence of the Sun and the word 'intelligence' is written underneath the symbol. Below this is a symbol like a broken fork, which represents the Spirit of the Sun, and the word 'spirit' is written within it. Finally, in the upper right-hand corner is the Seal of the Sun with the word 'seal' written within it. The Reverend Garnett thought that all of the symbols of the sun indicated that the charm was intended to be put in operation on a Sunday, which is the day of the Archangel Michael, as well as of the Sun. The actual words of the charm are written in cipher. It is fourteen lines long – the first three appearing to be an incantation of random words of power supposed to be efficacious against malevolent spirits and to protect against evil generally:

> *Apanton +hora + camab +naadgrass + pynavett ayias + araptenas*
> *+ quo + signasque +payns [pagus?] + sutgosikl + tetragrammaton +*
> *Inverma + amo + [symbol for Theos, God] + dominus + dues + hora + [hole in paper]*
> *+ fiat + fiat + fiat +*

The rest of the charm, in Latin, comprises biblical quotations:

> As it is said in the 17th chapter of St Matthew, 20th verse, 'By faith ye may remove mountains, be it according to (my) faith – if there is, or ever shall be enchantment or evil spirit that haunts or troubles this person, or this place, or these cattle, I adjure thee to depart, without disturbance, molestation or the least trouble – in the name of the Father and of the Son and of the Holy Ghost.'

The charm found at West Bradford in 1825. Its present location is unknown

Closing the charm is the Lord's Prayer in Latin (the *pater noster*), ending with the word *fiat*, meaning 'let it be done'.

After composition, the charm was carefully folded, and the words *Agla— On-Tetragrammaton* written in cipher on the outside. The first two words are names given to God by Jewish Cabalists, and the use of the third – Tetragrammaton – is intended to demonstrate that the person who made the charm knew what he was doing. As W. Self Weeks said in 1910, 'to show that it is the production of an artist who understood his business; for tetragrammaton (the sacred and unpronounceable name of Jehovah) and *fiat* are words of such potency, that a charm without them would be of no efficacy whatsoever.' [16]

I have examined the charm discovered at West Bradford in some detail because it appears to have been a 'stock' charm, several examples of which have turned up in the Pendle, Ribble Valley and Rochdale areas. It seems to have been utilised as an 'all purpose' protection charm. Other virtually identical charms were discovered in the rafters of a shippen in Healey, Rochdale in 1876,[17] and another under a brass plate on an old tombstone somewhere in Lancashire in about 1830.[18] This last example is most unusual in that it appears to be intended to protect a person from the attentions of evil spirits after his or her demise. It is a pity that details about this particular charm are so very vague as its use in this way appears to be unique.

King James I might furnish a clue to the motive in his book *Daemonologie*. When discussing the types of spirits that may be harnessed by witches, their methods of entering houses, and the forms they assume, the king comments, 'For if they have assumed a deade bodie, whereinto they lodge themselves, they can easely inough open without dinne anie Doore or Window, and enter in thereat.' [19] King James therefore believed that evil spirits could reanimate a corpse and move silently to enter the houses of the innocent to carry out the will of the witch. Why a reanimated dead corpse (sounding disturbingly like a clumsy old zombie) should be able to move around a house silently is not explained by His Paranoid Majesty. However, his comment probably explains the motive for concealing this charm against evil spirits within a tomb. Nobody wanted a dead relative prowling the earth under the control of a witch.

Another version of the same charm was discovered, probably by a Mr Charles Green, under a leather square at Daubers' Farm, Foulridge near Colne, in 1914.[20] The manuscript was discovered in a press bed. These beds were placed in little secret areas disguised as wardrobes or concealed behind bookshelves. They were warm and private, especially when they had curtains drawn across them or were fully enclosed with door panels. In this case the charm was presumably deployed to protect someone from evil spirits and nightmares while they were asleep, and therefore vulnerable to attack.

Finally, in the nineteenth century, a fragmentary copy of this popular charm seems to have been in the possession of Mrs Heaton, a noted local historian of Burnley. A photograph of the charm reproduced in the Transactions of the Burnley Literary and Scientific Society[21] shows that a substantial part of the middle section is missing along with some lines at the foot of the page. This one may be slightly different, for though it has the solar emblems and the seal of St Michael, it does not appear to have the same symbols in the magic square. At the time of writing no further details about this version of the charm are available, as the article accompanying the reproduction of the charm bizarrely makes no mention of it whatsoever. The whereabouts of Mrs Heaton's effects are unfortunately unknown which is a pity as she was evidently an enthusiastic collector of magical curiosities.[22]

The appearance of so many versions of the same charm in different locations in Lancashire indicates that this was a very popular charm and one used for any and every occasion that required protection. It is also a possibility that all the charms were produced by the same wise-man or woman. This does, however, seem a little unlikely, bearing in mind the distance involved between the Pendle area and Rochdale. We know that some wise-men certainly travelled around a great deal, but it is also indicated in the sources that practically every village in Lancashire had its own person skilled in the art of conjuring and white witchcraft. We should probably envisage a scenario involving many wise-men and women, all using the same charms copied over and over again, who passed them down through the generations. It is certainly the case that many of the charms discovered in Lancashire seem to have originated in Reginald Scot's *The Discoverie of Witchcraft* and similar books.

The Paracelsian Charm

A popular and well-used charm that certainly featured in Scot's inadvertent grimoire has been discovered in several locations. This was the well known protective talisman referred to as the Paracelsian charm after the famous sixteenth-century occultist Paracelsus. Scot's version runs thus:

A charme to drive awaie spirits that haunt anie house

Hang in everie of the foure corners of your house this sentence written upon virgine parchment; 'Omnis spiritus laudet Dominum: Mosen habent & prophetas: Exurgat Deus et dissipentur inimici ejus.' [23]

Translated, the three Latin sentences, which are Bible quotations, read: 'Let everything that breathes (has a spirit) praise the Lord (Psalms, 150); They have Moses and the Prophets (Luke 16); Let God arise, let his enemies be scattered.' (Psalms 64)

A good example of the Paracelsian charm turned up during work on Walden Cottage (originally a row of three cottages now knocked into one) when workmen were demolishing a fireplace. A further interesting find of a twelfth-century gold coin was made during the installation of a septic tank just outside the same property.[24] Walden Cottage lies in Sabden Fold, near Newchurch-in-Pendle, and is very close indeed to Bull Hole Farm where Demdike and Chattox had been active. It is also close to Moss End, the possible home of the alleged witches John and Jane Bulcock. The charm is written on parchment with two magical signs and the words:

Omnum	x	Spiritus
Laudent	x	Dominum
Mecum	x	Hebant
Prophetus	x	Exurgat
Deus x ut	x	Dis x x
Sipentur	x	Minimum[25]

If we compare Reginald Scot's version with the above, we can see that this is an extremely mangled version of the charm, presumably as a result of being copied over and over again through the centuries with no idea as to the meaning of the Latin words.

The two magical signs at the top of the charm are a little puzzling. The one on the right looks as if it may be an attempt at the Seal of the Sun, while that on the left resembles nothing more than a child's doodle, but may be an attempt at the Seal of Mars.

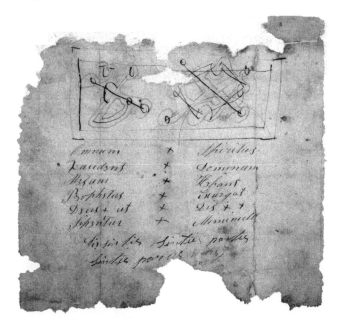

Paracelsian Charm found at Walden Cottage in Sabden Fold (Reproduced courtesy of Lancashire Record Office)

Two other very similar charms have been discovered in the Rochdale area. The first was handed to James L. Maxim in 1919 by a Mr Fred Kearsley. It had been found placed into a groove in the lintel of a small doorway while pulling down an old farm building at Cross Lees, Syke.[26] This building lies fairly near to Healey, where the discovery of another charm has already been described.

The Syke charm was folded along the whole length twice and then folded again at right angles and rolled up into a little packet. It was then wrapped carefully in thin lead foil, which is most unusual as this metal was normally, as I mentioned earlier, associated with cursing and malevolent magic rather than protective magic. When unwrapped, the parchment itself contained the remains of an unidentified light sea-green powder. This indicates the original presence of a small bronze object that had rusted away over the years – possibly something like a pin.

Not very long after the discovery of the Syke charm, Mr Maxim was informed that another similar charm had turned up a few years earlier at Meadow Head, near Wolstenholme Hall, Norden. This farm lies about two and a half miles north west of Rochdale, by the side of the Edenfield Road, and had been erected by 1775. What makes this perhaps the most fascinating charm of all is that it was again folded several times into a small packet, rather than being enclosed in lead, this particular example was sealed with a small piece of red wax. The piece of wax bore the actual fingerprint of the wise-man who produced the charm. It thus affords a delightful link with an actual individual who was practising white magic for a living in the eighteenth century.

After the parchment had been sealed it was then placed in a slot cut into a beam of the attic, and then plastered over to conceal it completely. When opened up, the charm proved virtually the same as that discovered at Syke.[27]

In common with the more elaborate protective charms discovered at West Bradford and elsewhere, it seems fairly clear that the Paracelsian charm as employed at Sabden Fold, Syke and Meadowhead, Rochdale were bought from wise-folk as another 'cure all' to repel the influences of evil spirits (i.e. witches' familiars and the fair folk), and in particular to prevent them from entering the building. The farmer and his wife would hope thus to protect themselves against their milk turning sour, butter refusing to 'come', bewitchment of their cattle and the undermining of their own health and good luck. As we have seen, in order to be effective Scot prescribed that the charm be hung in all four corners of the building, so it is possible that three other copies of the charm remained undiscovered in the three properties.

One of the possible reasons why this was such a popular charm was because

Portrait of the Renaissance occultist Paracelsus after whom the Paracelsian charm was named

it was so brief and would therefore have been a very cost effective product. We have to remember that most of the clients had no clue what was written on the piece of paper they had bought and therefore had no idea how much work had been involved in producing it. It was often a rather convenient part of the magic that the contents of the manuscript remained a secret. Indeed it seems to have been a custom with sellers of charms that they actually cautioned their customers against opening the charm up and reading it. William George Black tells the story of a young London woman who bought a toothache charm. It was found to read:

> *Good devil, cure her,*
> *And take her for your pains.*[28]

It is curious that the charms described above (all of which would appear to be eighteenth-century versions of much older charms) originate from either the Pendle or the Rochdale area. This might represent a local reaction to the high level of witchcraft accusations or suspicions in these particular areas over the years. The Pendle cases are well known (and more numerous than have been recorded previously), but Rochdale, although not on the same level, nonetheless had a number of its own relatively high-profile cases. In 1597, a pardon was granted to Alice Brerely of Castleton who had been condemned to death for murdering James Kershaw and Robert Scholefield by witchcraft.[29] In 1623

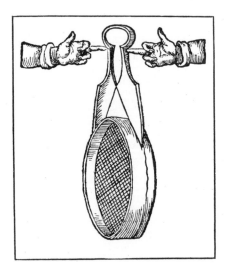

Divination using a sieve and shears

another Rochdale witch – Anne Butterworth of Butterworth – got lucky when she was found not guilty of witchcraft.[30] In 1641, Alice Scofield of Castleton was investigated for witchcraft when she was accused of predicting the identity of wrongdoers by means of a sieve and shears.[31]

In 1680 we hear of a Mary Turner of Moorhouse *infra* Butterworth who was accused of witchery[32] and in 1790 a lady called Janet Lord who lived in Packer Meadow was thought to be a witch. In 1881, W. Robertson recorded a strange story about Janet, who was a very peculiar-looking woman that muttered to herself constantly. A local gentleman who thought she had bewitched him called in a wise-man called Jemmy Whitehat of Heywood for help. The wise-man gave the 'victim' a charm that would ensure that the witch would be 'frizzled alive'. Some days later Janet Lord was found in her bed burned to death. Some put the bizarre turn of events down to Whitehat's effective magic, while others suggested murder. Whatever the truth, Janet Lord's cottage was from that time reputed to be haunted, remaining empty for many years until it was eventually converted into a hat factory.[33]

More Lancashire Charms

A seemingly unique astrological charm against witchcraft was discovered over the doorway of a house near Burnley. Designed to protect the house against evil spirits and burglary, and as a plea for money and good health, it runs thus:

Sun, Moon, Mars, Mercury, Jupiter, Venus, Saturn, Trine, Sextile, Dragons Head, Dragon's tail [astrological terms], I charge you all to gard this house from all evil spirits whatever, and gard it from aney thing being taken wrangasly, and give this family good Ealth & Welth.[34]

Unfortunately there is no indication in the source as to whether this charm was written upon the wall or on parchment and concealed above the door. Another splendid anti-witchcraft charm that was found in Simonstone at the end of the nineteenth century is worth noting, as it attempted to mention anything at all that might have evil designs on the building concerned.

> I abjure, and conjure you spirits, Analus, Anla, Annala, Anner, Anagankur, or three Belphorus, in the name of God the Father, God the Son, God the Holy Ghost, to make either a witch, witches, wizard, or wizards, blast, or blasts, evil eye or decietful [sic] tongue, sorcerer or cunjeror, to burn and consume to atoms every individual belonging to the diabolical art of Witchcraft that is made use of to work iniquity upon the body of--- or any of his family. For the sake of Christ. Amen.[35]

Again, it is a terrible pity that we are not told where this charm was found in Simonstone, under what circumstances, or what form it took. There is more than a note of hysteria in its tone, and this may be a DIY charm in response to a specific threat rather than one supplied by a local wise-man, although the use of impressive-sounding words of conjuration might suggest a certain level of magical knowledge, if a rather a dubious one. Belphorus might, at a pinch, be identified

The demon Belphegor
(Dictionnaire Infernal, 1863)

with Belphegor, a demon whose name derives from Baal-Peor, a Moabite mountain god. Analus, and the variations of the name that follow, are a bit of a puzzle but may be intended for Anani, a fallen angel.

Finally, we cannot ignore a simply splendid Lancashire anti-witch charm that bears little resemblance to those already discussed. A copy was found amongst the effects of an old farmer, some time prior to 1964. Like the Rochdale charms, it was folded into a little packet and was secured by three black seals (presumably of wax), into each of which were impressed the hackle of a red cockerel. Mr F. Kirkby of 934 Burnage Lane, Levenshulme, Manchester, drew attention to the existence of this manuscript when he sent a copy to the publication *The Dalesman* in 1964. I am indebted to the editor for providing a copy of this letter and accompanying illustrations.[36]

Mr Kirkby commented that he understood that the charm was fastened above the rear door of the farm as the front door was sealed up and never used. A couple of comments may be ventured upon. Around the outside of the protective six pointed star (the star of David rather than a pentagram) are the sentences: 'In him shall be the strength of thy hand. He shall keep thee in six troubles Yea even in seven shall no harm come to thee'. While the first sentence has eluded identification, the second is perhaps a biblical quotation as it seems to be an adaptation of the Book of Job 5/19: 'He shall deliver thee in six troubles: yea in seven there shall no evil touch thee'.

Other elements include fairly stock words of power, e.g. *Sadai* and *Adonai*, however there is also the interesting reference to *Nalgah*. This particular entity is one of the seven 'good angels' that watch over mankind to keep them from harm. Appropriately enough, *Nalgah's* particular responsibility is to protect those who

A farmhouse charm, published in The Dalesman, 1964

are being assaulted by evil spirits and witches, by strengthening the resolve of those inflicted by such troubles. His appearance is suitably heavenly, as he wears a golden crown, and he is represented as being armed with a spear and shield to protect the victims of *maleficia*.[37]

The trial of the Lancashire witches ensured that Lancastrians continued to suffer from 'witchcraft paranoia' for centuries after the 1612 executions. The wise-folk must have worked overtime to allay fears and produce charms to defend property and persons against *maleficia*. Occasionally however, the decent God-fearing people of Lancashire felt the need to take more pro-active measures. These were the people who became paranoid because nothing went right for them, be it illness, general bad luck or lack of money. They interpreted every-thing as a witch attack. To make matters worse, it was often the case that the identity of the supernatural tormentor was unknown. Under these circumstances something really powerful was needed – something that would not only identify the witch in question but with any luck would kill her as well. It was fervently anticipated that during this particular procedure the witch might reveal herself by rushing to the house of the victim to put a halt to the torment. This would give the victim the chance to scratch her and draw blood and thus remove her spell. When it was an emergency case, the local wise-man would often recommend a tried and tested way of identifying and disposing of a troublesome witch – the deployment of a 'witch bottle'.

Witch Bottles and Unpleasant Ingredients

The idea of a witch bottle was that you took a container (which could be anything from an ordinary glass bottle to an elaborate stoneware Bellarmine jug) and into it you placed sharp items such as nails and pins alongside personal items associated with the bewitched victim. These could include nail parings and hair. By far the most important ingredient, however, was the victim's urine. Heart-shaped pieces of felt (which, it is thought, were intended to identify the witch bottle with the physical body of the witch) pierced with pins were also included in some examples. This of course brings to mind the animal hearts pierced with pins that I have already described.

The witch had already established a magical link by casting a spell on the victim in the first place. Witch bottles were therefore a means of enabling the victim to turn the tables by exploiting this personal link to his or her own advantage. The witch (even if her identity was unknown) was rendered vulnerable to attack by the victim, and the witch's own *maleficia* could be thrown back at her through the medium of the victim's body parts and fluid.[38]

An early reference to the efficacy of urine combined with pins as a weapon against a witch is given in George Gifford's *Dialogue Concerning Witches* (1593): 'The cunningman biddeth, set on a posnet or some pan with nayles, and saeth [seeth] them [in the urine] and the witch shall come in while they be in saething, and within a fewe days after, her face will be all bescratched with the nailes.' There may be a potential link here between the above remedy and the belief that scratching a witch and drawing blood would counteract her spell.

Before contemporary references to its use in witch bottles made the concept familiar, urine had already been regarded as a potent protective substance for many years. It continued to be regarded as such into modern times and has been credited with many medicinal and antiseptic qualities. Along with Gandhi, Moraji Desai – president of India during the 1970s – was a great believer in drinking a small quantity of his own urine every day. The unconventional actress Sarah Miles is also a devotee of this practice. In eighteenth-century Scotland it was the custom to sprinkle the horses and plough with urine at the start of the ploughing season, while women would sprinkle family members with it on New Year's Eve, which can hardly have made them very popular. It is also interesting to note that fairies were said to find urine extremely offensive, for which one can hardly blame them!

Urine was also used in alchemy and led to the discovery of a new element by German alchemist Henig Brand in about 1669. While attempting to turn base metal into silver using concentrated urine, he produced by mistake a glowing substance called phosphorus (from the Greek for 'light bearing'). He kept his new substance a secret while attempting to use it to turn base metal into gold. Needless to say he failed miserably.

Once the witch bottle had been prepared according to the instructions of a wise-man, and all the personal items were safely secured within, there were two main methods of using it to attack the witch. The first, and the most extreme, involved corking it securely and then heating it over the fire until it exploded. In 1681 the Oxford puritan Joseph Glanvill describes this method in *Sadducismus Triumphatus*. In his story, a gentleman was very concerned about his bewitched wife and called in a local wise-man who:

> … therefore advised him to take a Bottle, and put his Wife's Urine into it, together with Pins and Needles and Nails, and Cork them up, and set the Bottle to the Fire, but be sure the Cork be fast in it, that it fly not out. The Man followed the

Prescription, and set the Bottle to the Fire well corkt, which, when it had felt awhile the heat of the Fire, began to move and joggle a little, but he for sureness took the Fire shovel and held it hard upon the Cork. And as he thought, he felt something one while on this side, another while on that, shove the Fire shovel off, which he still quickly put on again, but at last at one shoving the Cork bounced out, and the Urine, Pins, Nails and Needles all flew up, and gave a report like a Pistol, and his wife continued in the same trouble and languishment still.

In this particular instance, the method of heating the bottle resulted in the cork blowing out and the failure of the operation. Had the bottle blown apart as intended, then it would, with any luck, have resulted in the death of the witch.

In the above story, there seemed to be a little uncertainty as to what had actually been trapped inside the bottle, and it may have been thought that the witch's familiar had been drawn into the receptacle. The man commented that he felt something in the bottle actually moving about and trying to push his fire shovel away from the cork. This certainly sounds as if there was a physical and spiritual presence in the witch bottle fighting back. Indeed the wise-man commented on the failure of the operation, 'It seems it was too nimble for you.' [39]

It might be instructive here to look at the confession of Margaret Johnson, accused of witchcraft in the second major Lancashire outbreak in 1634. Margaret said, 'The [familiar] spirit tells them when and where the meeting must be, and if a witch desires to be in any place suddenly, her spirit will convey her thither, or into a room in a man's house, but it is not the substance of her body that goes into such room, but her spirit that assumes shape and form.' [40]

This would seem to indicate that it was believed that both the familiar spirit and the essential spirit (soul?) of the witch travelled abroad together. We have come across this idea before, when James Device joined with his familiar spirit Dandy to murder John Duckworth of The Laund. It may be, therefore, that both entities were crashing around in the witch bottle of Glanvill's story. We are often left wondering about these finer points of contemporary belief. How the witch bottle, the witch herself and her familiar spirit interacted is a question that continues to challenge current scholarship.

Be that as it may, the wise-man of Glanvill's story next prescribed the use of another witch bottle, prepared in the same way as the first, but to be employed in a slower and safer manner. This bottle he instructed the concerned husband to

Witch bottle found at Back Lane, Trawden (Image courtesy of Cliffe Castle Museum, Keighley)

bury under the ground. It was thought that the witch attacked in this way would be unable to 'make water' (i.e. pass urine), and presumably the intention was that he or she should die of acute kidney failure. The burying of this particular witch bottle resulted, we are told, in the recovery of the wife and the death of a 'wizzard' from a town some miles away. Therefore it was a happy ending for all concerned (apart from the deceased wizard, of course).

Well over two hundred examples of witch bottles have come to light in the British Isles, all of which had been buried. Those which had been heated to the point of explosion would naturally leave no trace in the archaeological record.

Favourite places for burying witch bottles that were designed for human use seem to have been under the hearth of the home, beneath the threshold, below floorboards or occasionally up the chimney. As with written charms, many witch bottles, no doubt, have been destroyed by the finder over the years as a result of superstitious dread and ignorance. These containers – which came in all sorts of shapes and forms – and their ingredients, look very much like examples of malefic magic and strictly speaking, of course, this is exactly what they were. The fact that the black magic was being practised against a witch is really neither here nor there.

Sometime in the nineteenth century, a president of the Burnley Literary and Scientific Society told members that he had found a bottle full of pins buried in the graveyard of St Mary's Church, Newchurch-in-Pendle. He considered it had been put there to work some evil, and evidently had no knowledge of the functions of a witch bottle. We are left wondering what he was doing digging around in a graveyard in the first place! [41]

A good example of an intact and sealed stoneware witch bottle was discovered under floorboards at Back Lane, Trawden by a Mr Stanley Cookson of Golden Square – in 1956 or thereabouts. Mr Cookson commented that the house in which the bottle was found was marked on the map as the 'site of ancient barn and shippen', which, he says, was presumably later converted into a cottage. Further enquiries established that the bottle was buried in an upright position and contained 4 handmade nails, 3 parts of broken steel, a tangled, compressed ball of hair and 'an unknown liquid'.[42] I think by now we can guess the identity of the liquid!

Trawden is, of course, a very fitting place in which to discover an anti-witch bottle. It was on her way to Trawden on a begging expedition that Alizon Device had her fateful, and ultimately fatal, encounter with John Law, the pedlar. Alizon probably begged at Trawden regularly, and she would have been well known in the village. The villagers of Trawden are not likely to have forgotten her in a hurry, and would have been constantly on the alert for further supernatural trouble.

In the wake of the 1612 trials, people all over Lancashire must have been casting around for ever more creative ways of protecting themselves against *maleficia*. We have seen that while a cross was considered good magic in the Christian mind, powerful older magic was represented by the deployment of iron. Logically, then, one of the most effective weapons against witches must have been the combination of iron either decorated with, or in the shape of a cross. In 1634, a very naughty boy who was fascinated by tales of the famous witches of 1612 took advantage of local paranoia to cause all manner of trouble. As a result all hell broke loose again in Pendle. This time, the witches of Lancashire attracted the attention not only of the local magistrates, but also of the King of England and the entire population of London, including its playwrights and theatre managers. It all started at a house with the curious name of Hoarstones where, in 1895, an iron cross was discovered, concealed within one of its walls ...

Following page: The meeting at Hoarstones, Illustration by Phiz, 1871

CHAPTER FIVE

King Charles I and the Supernatural Roadshow

What place is this? It looks like an old barn.
I'll peep in at some cranny or other
and try if I can see what they are doing. Such a bevy of beldames did
I never behold, and cramming like so many cormorants ... '[1]

O n 1st November 1633, young Edmund Robinson of Wheatley Lane – near the village of Fence in Pendle Forest – had a very exciting adventure. According to the story that he eventually related to King Charles I in London, he had been playing out and minding his own business when he was approached by two greyhounds. One of these dogs suddenly transformed itself into a neighbour called Frances Dicconson, while the other dog turned itself into a little boy. To Edmund's astonishment, Mrs Dicconson then changed the little boy into a horse by putting a magic bridle over his head. She and young Robinson mounted the horse-boy and rode him to a new house called Hoarstones, which was situated about a quarter of a mile away in the village of Fence. A great crowd of witches was assembling at the house on their horses. After tying their steeds to a hedge, they went into the house where a fire burned merrily. There, Edmund found himself taking part in a full-scale witch assembly and feast.

Edmund claimed to recognise several neighbours among this motley throng, including Henry Priestley's wife and son, Alice Hargreaves, Jennet Device, William Device, Holgate[2] and his wife of West Close, and several others. The witches offered Edmund food and drink, and then they all repaired to the nearby barn. Here, while some pulled horrible faces at Edmund, others yanked on ropes suspended from the beams. This had the effect of making further foodstuffs cascade down from the roof into waiting basins.[3] When he looked round and spotted three of the witches clutching clay dolls and sticking pins into them, he decided enough was enough and that it was time to take to his heels.

Raising hue and cry the witches, led by Mistress Lloynd, Mistress Dicconson and Jennet Device, chased the boy to a place called, aptly enough, Boggart Hole. A boggart is a species of Lancashire fairy that took various forms, none of them pleasant. According to *A History of the Parish of Fence*, published by the local parochial church council in 1937, this haunted spot may be identified with a property called Green Bank Farm which lies within easy running distance of the house at Hoarstones.[4] Here, instead of being accosted by an angry boggart and having that to deal with as well as witches, he was lucky enough to be saved by the arrival of two horsemen riding along the highway. Having spotted the riders, the witches abandoned the chase and Edmund hurried home.

Edmund the Witchfinder

Edmund and his father eventually reported this thrilling episode to local magistrates Richard Shuttleworth of Gawthorpe Hall and John Starkie of the neighbouring Huntroyde, on 10th February 1634 – a very suspicious three months after the event. As a result of young Robinson's allegations, many locals found themselves bogged down in a veritable quagmire of magical paranoia. Neighbour accused neighbour of witchcraft while Edmund himself soon achieved celebrity status. Set up as a famous 'witchfinder' by his father, the boy was taken round local churches to see if he could spot any more witches to add to his collection. These hag-spotting tours evidently ranged far and wide. At Kildwick in North Yorkshire, for example, the young witchfinder was observed one afternoon by John Webster, the young curate of the church. A later resident of Clitheroe and Master of its Grammar school (and, as we have seen, Vicar of Mitton), Dr Webster had a colourful career and has been described as a Grindletonian, puritan, physician and alchemist. He was the future author of the important work *The Displaying of Supposed Witchcraft* (1677) in which he described this particular outbreak of witchcraft in some detail.

In the above work he tells us that he was in Kildwick church this particular afternoon to preach, when Edmund, who looked to be about ten or eleven years old, was brought in and sat down upon a stall (presumably in the choir). While prayers were being said, Edmund looked round at everyone intently, no doubt causing members of the congregation to become rooted to the spot, eyes swivelling from side to side in acute discomfort. A little later, when Webster got the chance to ask the apprehensive church-goers what on earth was wrong, he was told that 'it was the Boy who discovered Witches'.

John Webster subsequently tried to question the boy at the house at which he and his father were staying, asking Edmund if he had really seen a witches' meeting or if someone had put him up to spinning this yarn. Edmund was swiftly plucked away from the young curate by his minders who bleated that even the magistrates hadn't asked the boy such an awkward question.[5] Webster replied that in that case they jolly well should have done. The boy was speedily removed from Webster's presence to continue his destructive work before the curate could say anything else, more's the pity.

According to a letter dated May 16th 1634, from Sir William Pelham to Edward Lord Conway, by this time at least 60 witches had been rounded up in Lancashire, and 19 had been condemned at the Spring Assizes in Lancaster.[6] The names of those denounced vary according to different sources, but the most reliable list would seem to be that included in the Londesborough manuscript. This particular record is also extremely important and informative because it not only lists the witches (20 in all) and the accusations made against them, but also includes details of the witch marks found on their bodies. This is a document of such importance to the history of Lancashire witchcraft that it is well worth while reproducing it here.

The Offenders condemned and accused for witchcraft with their marks at their attainder	The Evidences which were brought against them
1,2 Jane Hargrave vid'. & Alice ux' Henry Presley	for wasting and impairing the body of Jno. Moore
3 Jannet, ux. Henr: Hargraves Als Jacks wife. 1 mark in her secret place.	for killing a child in the belly of Ellen Robinson; for the death of Ellen ux. Rob. Smith; for the death of Isabell Mitton, vid'.
4 Jennet ux' Jno. Lownd of Pendle, three marks or paps In her secrets.	for killing Jam. Higgins, son of Edm. Higgins: for killing 2 kine, 1 horse of Jno. Sharples; 1 horse of Jno. Hargraves, 1 horse of Jno. Stevensons; & concerning a lewd p'te on a load of lyme.
5 Francisca, ux. Jno. Dicconson. 3 marks in her secrets.	for wasting and impairing the body of Edm. Stevenson.
6 Ellen, ux. Nichi Harsley als Brunsswicke. 1 mark or pap in her secrets	for killing of Barnard Parker
7 Jennet Device. 2 paps or marks in her secrets	for killing Isabell, ux' William Nutter.
8 Alce Higgins of Marsden, vid', no mark but a strong bone found on her in the gaol.	for killing Stephen Hargraves
9-11 Jno. Spencer, Mary, his wife. 1 pap on her hip; Mary their daughter 2 paps or marks in her secrets.	For wasting and impairing the body of Jno. Leigh
--Mary Spencer	For causing a pale or collocke to come to her full of water 14 yards up a hill from a well.
--p'd Jno. Spencer & Mary, his daughter	for killing Henry Roberts of Clevinger
--Jno. Spencer	for impairing the body of Sarah ux' George Frost; for dreaning & gelding a cowe new calved of Will'm Whittakers

--p'd Mary, ux' Jno. Spencer | for killing of one horse & divers beasts & cattle of one Nic. Cunclifts.

12–13 Robert Wilkenson, Jennet his wife, a foul mark or pap in her secrets, Mary ye wife & Mary his daughter [Spencers?]

for wasting and impairing by their practice of witchcraft the body of Edward Hartley

14 Mary Sheare als Shuttleworth, no ma'ke.

for killing Jennet, the wife of Richard Brewer, for impairing the body of Richard Brewer, his son, & for wasting the body of Alce Barcrofte.

15 Mary Aynsworth, 3 paps or marks in her secrets

for killing of Thomas Whittakers, an infant; for killing of Eliz: Whittakers, and for killing of George Cro'ckshawe, an infant.

16 Margrett Johnson, 1 mark or pap betwixt her seat & secrets

for killing of Henry Heape, for wasting & impairing the body of Jennet Shackleton.

17 Jennet Cronckshawe, 1 mark in her secrets

for laming and wasting ye body of Mary Pollard.

18 Isabell, ux' Jac. Hargraves, 1 mark or pap in her secrets

for killing Jennet, the wife of Edm. Robtishawe for spoiling of fleetings & curing them again.

--James Hargraves p'd Isabella ux' eius

for killing Jane, daughter of Lawrence Wilson

19 Christopher Pigles

for the death of Margrett Fields.[7]

20 Ellen Easthead als Woodpacke wife, against whom there is no evidence found, only in search a mark found of her body

Some of the above entries are of particular interest. Jennet Device, for example, may be the same Jennet who as a child sent her whole immediate family to the gallows in 1612. The Jennet mentioned above was accused of killing Isabell, the wife of William Nutter, and was found to have '2 paps (nipples) or marks in her secrets'. Mary Spencer, aged 20 of Burnley, was accused of helping her father John Spencer to murder Henry Roberts of Cliviger, and was also condemned 'for causing a pale or collocke to come to her full of water 14 yards up a hill from a well'.

Mary must be the only witch in history to be accused of having a bucket as her familiar spirit. Upon examination, the unfortunate Mary was found to have '2 paps or marks in her secrets'. Her father was also condemned for 'dreaning [draining of milk] and gelding a cowe new calved of William Whittakers.' This is a strange accusation until it is understood that gelding (normally, of course, associated with male animals) was also an old north country term for depriving a female animal of the power to reproduce. What lewd things Jennet Lloynd of Pendle (who had three witch marks) had been getting up to on a pile of lime, and why, is a fascinating question which may never receive a satisfactory answer.

Although she was found to have no witch mark, the above document tells us that Alice Higgin of Marsden was found to be in possession of a 'strong bone'. The meaning of this entry becomes clear when we examine the confession of Margaret Johnson dated 9th March: 'And she further saith, that such witches as have sharp boanes are generally for the devil to prick them with which have no papps or dug [nipples], but raiseth the blood from the place pricked with the boane, which withes are more great and grand witches than they which have papps or dugs.' [8] This discovery of a bone on Alice Higgins that confirms details in the confession of Margaret Johnson seems far too convenient to be true. We are probably quite justified in speculating that this 'discovery' of a strong bone on Alice's person was a either a total fabrication or the wilful misinterpretation of some innocuous bone object on the part of the gaoler, who still happened to be that experienced witch interrogator, Thomas Covell.

Like Alice Higgin, Margaret Johnson also hailed from Marsden. Nobody had actually come forward and accused her of witchcraft. She seems to have accused herself, and as a result became known by the nickname 'the penitent witch'. This was because she seemed fully convinced that she was a dangerous witch and therefore made a full and frank confession of her supernatural 'crimes' to anyone who would listen. Her confessions are very useful as they tell us what the ordinary person believed about supposed witch practices at this time. Margaret was found to possess one mark or pap 'between her seat and her secrets'.

Gawthorpe Hall, home to credulous J. P., Richard Shuttleworth

The Londesborough manuscript makes it quite clear that the condemned witches had at some point been subjected to the most invasive and humiliating 'body searches'. Where this examination took place is unclear. It may have been organised during their imprisonment at Lancaster. However, it is more than likely that they were searched during the preliminary procedures presided over by the credulous local magistrates, namely Richard Shuttleworth of Gawthorpe Hall and John Starkie of the neighbouring house, Huntroyde. These gentlemen may have instructed a 'jury of matrons' or possibly a local doctor to examine the accused witches, and the actual procedure could very easily have taken place at Gawthorpe Hall, being the most important manor house in the immediate area. The documents merely mention 'Padiham' as the centre of anti-witch operations. The women may, however, have been searched (while held under guard) in their own homes.

Sensible and sceptical John Webster, who had observed the Robinsons in action at Kildwick church, provides a reassuringly shocked contemporary comment on the practice of searching for witch marks in *The Displaying of Supposed Witchcraft*:

And the like in my time and remembrance happened here in Lancashire, where divers both men and women were accused for supposed Witchcraft, and were so unchristianly, unwomanly, and inhumanely handled, as to be stript stark naked, and to be laid upon Tables and Beds to be searched (nay even in their most privy parts) for these their supposed Witch-marks: so barbarous and cruel acts doth diabolical instigation, working upon ignorance and superstition, produce.[9]

Although found guilty by the jury at the Lancashire Assizes,[10] the judges expressed enough doubt about the verdicts to ensure that the executions of the condemned were respited, and the whole proceedings referred to the King in Council in London. King Charles I seems to have been fascinated by the case and ordered on 16th May that ' ... some of the principall and most notorious offenders amongst those persons which were lately tryed and condemned for Witchecraft and Sorcery, at the last assizes in the Countie of Lancaster, and afterwards reprieved should brought upp to attend his Majesty's further pleasure ... '[11] The king also specified their manner of travelling to the capital. The High Sheriff of Lancashire was to deliver them to the sheriff of the next county, and so on, until they reached London – rather like a bizarre game of pass the paranormal parcel. He also ordered John Bridgeman, Bishop of Chester, to examine the condemned prisoners prior to their departure for London. Edmund Robinson and his father were also summoned into the royal presence.

The witches originally chosen for the London trip were Margaret Johnson, 'the penitent witch', Mary Spencer of sentient bucket fame, Frances Dicconson who had allegedly taken Edmund to the Hoarstones 'sabbat', Jennet Hargreaves, John Spencer (Mary's father), Alice Higgin and Jennet Lloynd. We might comment here that if the Jennet Device involved in this case was the same one who sent her family to the gallows in 1612, then it is very strange indeed that the king expressed no desire to observe at first hand a young person already so celebrated and experienced in the ways of witchcraft. It may be, of course, that nobody had thought to inform the curious monarch that one of the accused witches was none other than the granddaughter of the infamous Mother Demdike.

The Magic Bucket

On 13th June, the Bishop of Chester finally arrived in Lancaster to examine the witches to find that only three of those whose presence the king had requested had survived the privations of Lancaster gaol. John Spencer, Alice Higgin and

Jennet Lloynd had died in prison and Jennet Hargreaves was 'sick past all hope of recovery'. Margaret Johnson must have been delighted to have someone else to talk at and the startled bishop was regaled with further details of her career as a hardened witch. In his report to the King's Council, the bishop hinted that her stories failed to agree with each other and that she obviously had an excellent imagination but a rotten memory! [12]

The tragic, young Mary Spencer defended herself vigorously and denied utterly that she had ever practised witchcraft. A regular churchgoer in Burnley before her arrest, she managed to repeat the creed and the Lord's Prayer. She described how she had often heard Mr Brierley (a famous member of the Grindletonian movement) preach and repeated what she had heard to her parents at home. The poor girl was now orphaned as both her mother and father had died in Lancaster gaol and had already been buried. She complained that her accuser, Nicholas Cunliffe, had borne a grudge against herself and her parents for several years.

It was no doubt with indignant and despairing sighs that she explained to the eminent churchman the truth behind one of the most bizarre accusations ever brought against a suspected witch – that of being able to make a bucket run to her down a hill. First of all, she explained, she did not actually hear this allegation of Cunliffe's at her trial because the crowd was so noisy [13] and the wind was so loud. This sounds very much as if there were holes in the roof of the court chamber, through which the wind was whistling noisily. While the Judges' Lodgings and Castle are known to have been in good repair in 1634, there are reports that the condition of the courthouse itself was often a matter of scandal, being so danger-ously ill-repaired that some judges had actually refused to hear cases there as they feared for life and limb. [14]

The truth behind the foolish story (as the accused witch said to the bishop) was that when she was a little girl, she used to go down to the well with her bucket, rolling it along beside her, trying to get ahead of it and playfully calling to it. Sometimes, of course, she managed to overtake the rolling bucket and so it looked as though she was indeed summoning it to come to her. That this childish game could ever have been interpreted as a criminal action serious enough to convict her as a witch, must have driven both Mary and her parents to utter despair.

Frances Dicconson was equally indignant at her condemnation and told the bishop that she had been set up by the young Edmund Robinson's father. He had promised to withdraw the accusation if her husband bribed him with 40 shillings. Her other accuser, Edmund Stevenson was, she claimed, also of bad character, being lately accused of felony.

Bishop Bridgeman sent his report to the king on 15th June and shortly afterwards the four women (including Jennet Hargreaves who had, it seems, recovered from her 'terminal' illness) set out for London and had arrived before the end of the month. In the capital the four suspected witches were not, as we might expect, immediately confined in a London dungeon but were instead given lodgings at the Ship Tavern. This may have been due to the inn being situated conveniently close to the royal palace at Greenwich. Once famous as the venue for ministerial dinners marking the end of each session of parliament, the Ship Tavern was regrettably destroyed by bombing in World War Two.[15] Its site is now occupied by the dry dock which houses the *Cutty Sark* clipper ship, which was badly damaged by fire during its restoration in 2007. Rather an unlucky spot, it would seem ...

Once the ladies had recovered from their journey and settled in, they must have been incredulous to discover just how famous they had become in London and even further afield. By this time they had become a favourite topic for gossip, not only among ordinary Londoners, but also members of the English aristocracy and even foreign royalty. A little earlier in the month, for example, an entry in Sir Thomas Brereton's diary (on 3rd June) tells us that he had been asked about 'the discovery of our Lancashire witches' by King Charles' sister, Elizabeth the 'Winter Queen' of Bohemia, who was at that time living in exile in The Hague. Elizabeth in turn regaled Sir Thomas with stories she had heard about a whole village full of witches at Westphalia, all of whom were 'deservedly burned'.[16]

At some point (it is not clear when) the witches were moved from what must have been relatively comfortable lodgings at the Ship to the notorious Fleet prison. First built in 1197, the Fleet was destroyed during the rebellion of Wat Tyler in the fourteenth century but swiftly rebuilt. Prisoners were kept in particularly foul conditions (often loaded down with chains and manacles) yet, in common with Lancaster gaol, were still charged rent for their accommodation in the dungeons. They were also expected to pay for their own food and drink. In Elizabeth's reign, for example, the fee for being held prisoner was 7/4d for a poor man, not including food. [17]

It is most unlikely that either King Charles or the Lancashire authorities would have been prepared to shell out for the board and keep of four convicted witches, under any circumstances. This may be one of the reasons why the authorities at the Fleet seized upon a 'wizard wheeze'. This was to charge Londoners an admission fee to the Fleet, where they could entertain themselves by staring at

the hapless witches in a sort of paranormal peep show. An outing to gawp at a real life captive witch from remote and uncivilised northern parts no doubt held great 'shiver' appeal for the Londoners. The funds created by the venture in all probability took care of their board and keep and may even have generated a healthy profit for the avaricious prison wardens. There was certainly no shortage of takers for tickets it would seem; Dr Webster informs us in *The Displaying of Supposed Witchcraft* that after the witches had arrived in London 'great sums were gotten at the Fleet to show them.'[18] As we shall see later, throughout the summer of 1634, playwrights jostled to get plays featuring the witches onto the London stage before their case had even been settled. In these plays, Mary's tame bucket became a comic turn, audiences gasped at the 'magic bridle' and transformation scenes, and a couple of the condemned witches appeared as characters under versions of their own names.

Frances, Margaret, Jennet and Mary were eventually examined formally (yet another humiliating full body search) on 2nd July and the following certificate was issued:

Surgeon's Hall in Monkwell Street, London
2nd July 1634,

We in humble obedience to your Lordship's command have this day called unto us the Chirurgeons and midwives whose names are hereunder written who have by the directions of Mr Dr Harvey (in our presence) made diligent search and inspection on those women which were lately brought up from Lancaster and find as followeth, viz:

On the bodies of Jennett Hargreaves, Ffrances Dicconson and Mary Spencer nothing unnatural or anything like a teat or mark or any sign that any such thing hath ever been. On the body of Margaret Johnson we find two things (which) may be called teats. The first in shape like to the teat of a bitch but in our judgement nothing but the skin as it will be drawn out after the application of leeches. The second is like the nipple or beat of a woman's breast, but of the same colour with the rest of the skin without any hollowness or issue for any blood or juice to come from thence.[19]

The above report was signed by ten midwives, by Alexander Reid, M.D. – the lecturer on Anatomy at the Barber Surgeons' Hall, whom William Harvey seems to have deputised to take his place – and by six other distinguished London surgeons.

The eminent Dr William Harvey, to whom the team reported, is famous for discovering the principle of circulation of the blood. He had been chief physician to King James and at the time of the witches' visit to London, held the position of 'physician-in-ordinary' to King Charles. A stubborn sceptic on the subject of witchcraft, his cynicism seemed to stem mainly from dislike of the idea that it credited power to women, all of whom he comprehensively disliked.

A fascinating seventeenth-century manuscript published in the *Gentleman's Magazine* of 1832 describes an encounter between Harvey and a witch in Newmarket, which took place sometime in the 1630s. This tells the story of the good doctor disguising himself as a wizard and visiting an old lady who lived in a lonely house on the edge of Newmarket Heath. Harvey managed to gain her confidence and get his foot in the door by telling the witch that he was a wizard and had come to talk to her about their 'common trade'. The woman believed him because, as he often commented to people, 'You know I have a very magicall face!' He then asked to meet her familiar, and the witch brought out a dish of milk and made a chuckling noise with her mouth, at which point a toad crawled out from under a chest and drank some of the milk.

Eager to examine the creature, Harvey handed the witch a shilling to go out and get some ale so that he could be left alone with it. Once he had got rid of the old lady he prepared to examine her familiar: 'His tongues [tongs] were ready in his hand, he catched up the toad in them; his dissecting knife was ready alsoe, he opened the toades belly, out came the milk. Hee examind the toades entrayles, heart and lungs, and it no ways differed from other toades, of which he had dissected many of, ergo it was a playne naturall toad'.

Having established to his own satisfaction that the toad possessed no magical attributes whatsoever, he concluded that the woman had tamed the toad by feeding it spiders and other reptiles or insects and had honestly come to believe it was a spirit and her familiar. On returning to the house and discovering the butchery of her pet toad, the woman 'flew like a tigris' at Harvey, scrabbling for his eyes and was, it seems, intent on permanently rearranging his face, or as the manuscript puts it, 'the good Doctor ... was in danger to have a more magical face than hee had before.' She refused to be mollified by money; whereupon Harvey was forced to tell her that he was the King's physician and had been sent to discover whether or not she was a witch and to have her arrested if she was. The old lady told him to go to the Devil and he finally managed to get out of the house without being subjected to any further GBH.[20] It is my considered opinion that Dr Harvey got away with it very lightly. If I had been the old lady I would have poured the ale all over his head before making every effort to turn him into a toad as a replacement for my pet. Alternatively I might have turned him into a cockroach and trodden on him.

It should come as no surprise after this story, then, that any team headed by this eminent and down-to-earth physician was unlikely to find anything out of the ordinary on the bodies of the Lancashire witches. Strange protuberances were noted, it is true, on the body of Margaret Johnson, but these were considered (presumably to her indignation) to be of natural origin. It does seem very curious indeed that while the Lancashire examination team established that Jennet Hargreaves, Frances Dicconson and Mary Spencer all possessed three witch marks in their private parts, the London physicians and midwives found nothing at all. On the other hand, the Lancashire authorities had found only one teat on the body of Margaret Johnson, while the London examination turned up two of them.

Shortly afterwards, we are told by John Webster that the witches were examined by King Charles and his Council. It is extremely difficult to imagine this encounter. Were the witches allowed to speak to the king? If so, did he understand a word they said? Did they understand a word the king said to them? Webster also tells us that the king issued a pardon to the four women, but there seems to be little supporting evidence for his assertion, even though the case against them had, by this time, more or less collapsed.

The Witches ate my Homework, Sir

Edmund Robinson and his father had been held separately in London in close confinement since the beginning of June 1634. Sometime at the beginning of July the young Edmund finally came clean to the king's coachman that he had made up the whole story of the witch meeting at Hoarstones. No doubt he felt under increasing pressure, with a constant barrage of questions being fired at him by extremely important people, not least being the king himself. The full truth about the alleged witch assembly at Hoarstones came out when Edmund eventually made a full confession to George Long, the Justice for Middlesex.

The long shadow of Demdike, Chattox and the other witches of 1612 had, it seems, fallen upon those persons accused of witchcraft in 1634. For Edmund, fascinated by the original witch stories, confessed that he had heard all about the Good Friday meeting at Malkin Tower back in 1612 and it was upon these very stories from twenty years before that he had based most of his own fabrications about the witches' Sabbat at Hoarstones. One of the reasons this particular house had suggested itself to him as a good venue was because he had been with his father at Hoarstones when he was building it for Thomas Robinson (no relation) to live in. He admitted that he had made up the whole tale of being abducted by Mrs Dicconson and other neighbours as a typical schoolboy excuse, because he had been playing out with friends when he was supposed to be bringing home his father's cattle.[21]

However, it would seem that things were not quite as clearly cut as this confession might indicate. For although Edmund certainly admitted he had made up the exciting stories about the shape-shifting witch, his abduction and the gathering of the witches, it would seem that the women concerned were already genuinely suspected of witchcraft. And it was due to this fact that he had chosen these particular women to be the stars of his tall story. Edmund informed the Justice, for example, that he had heard Edmund Stevenson complain about being 'troubled by' Frances Dicconson during his illness. He also heard Robert Smith say that when his wife was on her deathbed, she had accused Jennet Hargreaves of bewitching her to death. He added that William Nutter's wife was sure that Jennet Device and William Device, her half-brother, had bewitched her. Lloynd's wife, he had heard, had been accused of bewitching to death a cow of Sharpee Smith. As Edmund emphasised, 'and thereupon he framed these tales concerning the persons aforesaid because he heard the neighbours repute them for witches'.[22]

Therefore, although Edmund made up the story about a witch meeting that he later confessed to be phony, this did not alter the fact that some of those condemned had actually been accused of the usual *maleficia*, i.e. supernatural murder and the bewitching to death of animals. It is therefore hard to see why those accused of these particular crimes should have received any pardon from the king.

No Escape

This may provide one of the reasons why the women starring in the Lancashire Supernatural Roadshow in London were not immediately set free and sent back to their homes. For we find that in late summer they were herded from London straight back to Lancaster Castle where they continued to be held prisoner in the company of the other condemned witches. On the occasion of William Farington of Worden's appointment as High Sheriff of Lancashire in 1636, a calendar that represented a sort of prison stocktaking exercise was compiled.

A calendar of the names of the Prysoners remaining and beinge in his Md Goale and Castle of Lancaster this assizes being the xxij daie of August 1636

> Robert Wilkinson
>
> Jennet His wife
>
> Marie Shuttleworth
>
> [Presumably Mary Sheare]
>
> Jennet Device
>
> Alice Priestley

[not mentioned in the Londesborough list but mentioned as Henry Priestley's wife by Edmund Robinson]

Jennet Cronkshawe

Marie Spencer

Jennet Hargreaves

Ffrances Dicconson

Agnes Rawsterne [23]

[This final name is unfamiliar]

Two years after their London adventure, Mary Spencer, Jennet Hargreaves and Frances Dicconson were therefore right back where they started, facing a bleak and hopeless future in the grim dungeons of Lancaster gaol. It is interesting to note that Jennet Device was included in the list of those still mouldering away in the castle at this time. An interpolated burial entry in the records of St Mary's, Newchurch-in-Pendle, reads, 'Jennet Sellar alias Devis sepult. 22nd December 1635'.[24] It has been suggested that this entry records the burial of the same Jennet Device who was a child witness in the 1612 case. If this is so, then the Jennet Device listed as being a prisoner at Lancaster in 1636 cannot possibly be the same Jennet Device who sent her family to the gallows. Even a witch cannot fool us into thinking she was both dead and buried at Newchurch in 1635 yet being held prisoner in Lancaster Castle a year later! Alternatively of course, the Jennet Device recorded as a prisoner at Lancaster is indeed the famous one, and the one buried at Newchurch merely has a similar name.

For what it is worth, I consider it suggestive that Jennet's mother, Elizabeth Device, was accused of having a bastard child with one Sellar. This might certainly indicate that the Jennet Sellar alias Devis buried in the graveyard of Newchurch in 1635 may be identified with the infamous Jennet Device who was sister of Alizon and James Device. Unfortunately, of course, this disposes of the satisfying notion that the child who accused her family of being witches received her just desserts by receiving an equally unfair conviction for the self-same crime.

Of Margaret Johnson – the penitent witch – there is no mention on the list of those still imprisoned in 1636. Possibly she had not survived a further two years in prison. She may even have failed to survive what must have been a tough journey back from the capital. The condemned witches appeared to be in limbo, regarded as neither guilty nor innocent. It is very likely that none of them could find anyone willing to act as surety for them and even more likely that they had no way of paying the gaoler's fees. If these remained unpaid, the prisoners were going nowhere. The Lancaster authorities were notoriously unsympathetic to the problems of prisoners who found themselves in financial difficulties – particularly when witchcraft was involved. A transcript of a document from the Lancashire Record Office makes the blood run cold and may throw more light on the predicament of these accused witches who seem to have been abandoned to their fate.

> *The Humble peticion of Ann Baker of Warrington*
>
> **Sheweth,**
>
> *That wheras your peticioner beinge imprisoned within the Comon Gayle or Castle at Lancaster upon the suspition of sorsorie or witchcraft and noething proueved against her, and remaineth heare still for not paying her feese wich shee can not procure, nor pay haveing noe frends to looke upon her but hath sould all her clothes, her hatt and aprine and all that shee hath, and now lieth sore sicke in bed and is not able to ster or to helpe her selfe any way.'*
>
> Oct. 1658

She goes on to ask the Justices to release her but their decision was that she should have 'Nothing'.[25]

The plight in which some of these prisoners found themselves is quite heart-rending. In spite of selling everything she had – including her hat and apron – in a vain attempt to pay her prison fees, this sick, friendless woman (who had been found guilty of no crime) received no assistance whatsoever. One can only hope that those responsible for such heartless decisions received some suitable 'karmic' reward. We do not know what happened to Ann, but it is difficult to avoid the assumption that she would only have been liberated from Lancaster gaol by her own death. It is more than likely that those accused by Edmund Robinson in 1634 found themselves in the same predicament as Ann Baker of Warrington, from which there appeared to be no avenue of escape whatsoever.

As 1637 drew to a close, we have a piece of evidence that suggests there was indeed no sign of light at the end of the tunnel for the condemned witches immured in the castle. At this time, a puritan called Henry Burton was having his own problems. After being pilloried and having his ears cut off in London, he was sent up north and imprisoned in Lancaster Castle. Here, he tells us, he was confined in a vast desolate room without furniture; if a fire was lit, smoke filled the room and the planks on the floor were so rotten he was in danger of falling though them to the room below.

Beneath him, he says, was a deep, dark chamber in which were immured five witches, one of whom had her child with her. He complains that they kept up a 'hellish noise' night and day, and grumbles that as the authorities had plenty of other places to put them, he did not see why he should have to put up with their constant racket.[26] (It might be uncharitable, but is nonetheless quite irresistible to observe that the noise may have been even worse if he was still in possession of a full set of ears!) Henry also comments that the witches had been in the castle for 'a very long time'. There had, however, certainly been others held in the gaol on suspicion of witchcraft since the outbreak of 1634.

We know from a couple of letters, for example, that Bishop Bridgeman had again been asked by the Secretary of State to examine four witches (this time from Wigan) in February 1635. He arrived at Lancaster sometime in May only to find two of them had died. The surnames of the two surviving witches were Swift and Barker. The latter, according to the bishop, had been reputed to be a witch for a long time and lived about a mile from his own house in Wigan.[27] The outcome of the case against the Wigan witches is unknown. It is possible, however, that they too found it impossible to gain release from the castle, and may easily have been among those witches who had aggravated Henry Burton so much in 1637.

It seems a strange and alien concept to us that one of the witches mentioned by Burton had her child with her, considering that she was living in such appalling conditions. According to Walter Bennett in *The History of Burnley*, Mary Sheare (or Shuttleworth) had an illegitimate son baptised at St Peter's church in 1626, and Jennet Cronkshaw gave birth to an illegitimate daughter in 1633.[28] The child in the deep dark dungeon of Lancaster Castle may have belonged to either of these women and its illegitimate status may explain why nobody on the outside was willing to take any responsibility for this youngster. The mind shies away from contemplation of its fate.

In contrast to the families whose lives he had comprehensively ruined, the young Edmund Robinson and his father got off scot-free and went home to Wheatley Lane in the position of being able to dine out on their exploits for many years to come. The young Edmund was still alive and kicking in the late 1670s when John Webster was writing his famous work on the subject of witchcraft. Known locally by then as Ned o' Roughs, Robinson had on several occasions described to Dr Webster how his father and several friends had encouraged him to persist in his witchcraft accusations so that they could gain monetary profit and revenge upon their neighbours. This sounds plausible enough, yet it is difficult to believe anything proffered as truth by this unpleasant individual. One wonders if he ever suffered one iota of remorse for the suffering and premature deaths for which he was undoubtedly responsible. We should probably conclude that he did not.

The Mysterious Hoarstones

A strange atmosphere may have clung to the house and land around Hoarstones even before it acquired its association with the practice of witchcraft. A reference to the name occurs in the Court Rolls of Clitheroe in 1547: 'Item they present on heigh way begynyng at Kynfeldclough yait to Heigham Lawe and so to the tenement of Edmund Emott, and so discending to a yait [gate] of Edmund Robynson thelder, and frome thense folowyng the nether side of a dyche above the Horestones, now in the holding of Edmund Robynson thelder ... to the tenement of the lait wyff of James Hergreaves ... '

There is no real indication in the above reference that there was a dwelling house at Hoarstones in the mid-sixteenth century. It is referred to merely as 'the horestones', held by Edmund Robinson the elder. We might remember that the young Edmund Robinson had spent some time watching his father build the house at Hoarstones for Thomas Robinson in 1633, and that it is described at that time as a new house. There seems to be little reason to suppose that this new house replaced one already existing on the site.

'The Horestones' in the mid-sixteenth-century reference probably refers to an actual stone feature. The hoarstone (se hara stan in Old English) is a common term for stones that were chosen as boundary markers because of their great age and distinctive grey appearance. As Michael Swisher comments, 'That the hoarstone existed in old English as a common concept can be seen in its meaning as a boundary marker in Anglo-Saxon charters ... Today in Great Britain one still finds ancient stone formations as well as individual stones bearing the name 'Hoar Stone'.[29]

*The Hore Stone, a chambered tomb at
Enstone in Oxfordshire
(Photo: Chris Collyers)*

We do not know what the original Hoarstones at Fence looked like, or what their original purpose was. It has been suggested that a prehistoric stone circle once existed there, traces of which could still be seen in the 1950s before they were covered over with rubbish. Unfortunately there seems to be no further reliable information about this fascinating possibility. However, there seems little doubt that an ancient, locally significant stone monument of some sort (be it a stone circle or ancient burial chamber) must once have existed in the vicinity of the house and after which the house itself was named.

As well as being utilised as geographical boundary stones, hoarstones also had a more unearthly association; it has been suggested that in Anglo-Saxon times they were thought to mark the boundary between the known world and the supernatural realms. Michael Swisher says:

An interesting, if easily overlooked, formulaic expression in Old English literature, se harne stan, 'hoar stone', indicates the boundary between the known, familiar world of human activity and the frightening realm of monsters, the supernatural and unusual adventure. The hero who sees this marker is forewarned and if he treads further, he does so with the knowledge that a normal struggle with an earthly foe must not be expected.[30]

Burial chambers, standing stones, stone circles and other prehistoric monuments were famously attractive to the fair folk and spirits of all kinds, and it is more than likely, therefore, that Hoarstones already had a bit of a reputation as a haunted spot. Edmund Robinson could not really have chosen a more suitable setting than the Hoarstones for his imaginary encounter with evil witches of the 'otherworld'.

The barn next to Hoarstones house, where, according to the story, the witches pulled on ropes to get food and stuck thorns into clay dolls, is no longer extant. By 1845, another, more substantial barn had been erected on the same site.[31] The house itself, built by Edmund Robinson's father for a wealthier and more respectable Robinson family in 1633, was heavily restored in 1895.

It was during this restoration that a cross fashioned out of iron was found concealed within one of the walls.[32] That the owner of Hoarstones sought the protection of cold iron need not surprise us. Although Robinson had admitted making up tales about the witches' feast in the house and adjoining barn, the fact remained that the men and women accused of meeting there never quite managed to clear their names. As Alison Findley says, 'Their fictional identity

Hoarstones House (Photo courtesy of Stuart Mason)

as a weird sisterhood outlived the evidence of their innocence.'[33] The neighbours might therefore have come to the conclusion that there was no smoke without fire and that Robinson might, just might, have been telling the truth after all. And so regardless of whether or not the stories were true, the house called Hoarstones would naturally acquire some notoriety as a location where witches met and feasted.

These were not just any old witches, but creatures glamorous and powerful enough to attract the attention of the king in London. Not only that, but their exploits had been deemed extraordinary enough to be capable of tickling even the jaded palates of the sophisticated London audiences. They had actually thought it worth paying out good money to gape at the Lancashire witches moping about in the Fleet and to watch their exploits dramatised on stage. Everybody was beginning to agree that there must therefore be something very special about Lancashire and the Pendle area in particular, which produced exceptionally potent witches.

Attitudes to the local witches began to diversify. While the fear of witchcraft continued to prevail among the less educated until within living memory, from 1634 onwards other sections of the population began to see the witches as a resource to be exploited for entertainment value. We would soon see Mother Demdike appearing alongside Mother Goose in pantomime and eventually even Charles Dickens would play tribute to the famous witches of Lancashire. And as time went on, fascination with the personalities of the witches became as powerful as the fear of their potential *maleficia*, and Lancashire was to become increasingly proud of its extraordinarily charismatic witches.

CHAPTER SIX

The Charm of the Lancashire Witches

She's a pride of beauty so bright,
Her image my fancy enriches;
My charmer's the village delight,
And the pride of the Lancashire witches.[1]

 shift in public perception seems to have begun as early as 1634, when Mary Spencer, Margaret Johnson and the other witches had a play written about them in which they were portrayed as comic characters. For the next couple of centuries the Lancashire witches – broomsticks in hand – delivered to their audiences not only shivers and shudders but also merriment and fun as they sang and danced around the stage.

Inspired no doubt by the success of the witches in Macbeth, two playwrights named Heywood and Brome wrote a play about the witches of 1634 when they were still in prison in London. *The Witches of Lancashire* (published as *The Late Lancashire Witches*)[2] was performed by the King's Men at the Globe theatre for three days on 11th to 13th August, 1634.[3] We are most fortunate in that we actually have a contemporary 'review' of this play, which was considered a huge success in its time not only among the *hoi polloi* who usually enjoyed such frolics, but also among the 'fine folke' of London.

Nathaniel Tomkyns was in the audience at the Globe and described the play in detail, including fascinating special effects such as live birds being released from pies on stage.[4] Tomkyns also mentioned the staging of the Hoarstones feast with food being produced when the witches pulled on ropes, and the 'walking of pailes of milke by themselves' – a reference, of course, to Mary Spencer's tame supernatural bucket. The play was essentially a comedy. They were all-singing, all-dancing witches playing what were portrayed as 'mischievous tricks' on their victims rather than engaging in serious *maleficia*. 'Tis all for mirth, we mean no hurt,' insisted Mistress Generous, their fictional leader.[5]

1634 also saw the publication of two ballads, *Prophane Pastime or the Witches Mad Humors* and *The Witches' Dance*, both of which are now lost, but that probably featured the topical witches of Lancashire.[6] Two further ballads dating from the reign of Charles II are still extant. In *News from Hyde Park* (*c*. 1660), a fashionable lady taking off her make-up was compared to a Lancashire witch: 'She washed all the paint from her visage, and then/She look'd just (if you will believe me)/Like a Lancashire Witch of fourscore and ten ... '[7] While another extant ballad of the time, which may be an extract from a contemporary play, is entitled *The Lancashire Witches*, there seems to be no reference to Lancashire in any of its eleven verses and its provenance is a little vague.[8]

The Lancashire witches also figure in what is believed to be the earliest English playbill still in existence. It is thought to date from about 1655 when the theatres were closed by spoilsport Oliver Cromwell, but puppet shows seemed to be tolerated. The playbill advertised a show being held in John Harris' Booth on the occasion of Bartholomew Fair in London. This took place on and around 24th August each year. The performance featured ' ... the merry humours of Punchinello and the Lancashire Witches ... Acted by Figures as large as Children two years old.' This appears to be the first mention of Mr Punch in England and his association with the witches probably suggests another comic treatment of the subject.[9]

Mother Demdike takes the Stage

A play first written and produced in 1681 was to remain popular until well into the eighteenth century. It was written by one Thomas Shadwell and went by the less than snappy title of *The Lancashire Witches and Teague O Divelly the Irish Priest: A Comedy*. This play was staged originally at The Duke's Theatre at Lincoln's Inn Fields and later at the Theatre Royal on Drury Lane. In common with Heywood and Brome's earlier play, the piece had plenty of music and dancing and this type of entertainment was often described as a 'semi-opera'. Such works combined spoken plays with masque, and the music – in this case written by a Mr John Barrett – was usually limited to moments in the play devoted to love scenes or the supernatural.[10] In the seventeenth century, the roles of supernatural hags were traditionally played by the adult male comedians in the theatre company.

THE

Lancashire VVitches,

AND

Tegue o Divelly

THE

Irish PRIEST.

A

COMEDY

Part the First.

THE

Amorous Bigot,

with the Second Part of

Tegue o Divelly

A

COMEDY.

Both Acted by their Majesties Servants.

Written by *Thomas Shadwell* Poet Laureat, and Historiographer Royal to their Majesties.

London, Printed for *R. Clavell*, *J. Robinson*, *A.* and *J. Churchill* and *J. Knapton*, and are to be Sold at the *Crown* in St. *Pauls* Church-yard, 1691.

The songs delivered by the witches might therefore have been delivered in deliberately discordant deep voices. Alternatively, the men may have sung in shrieking falsetto, to add a further comic element to the play.[11]

Shadwell's play is significant to us because it introduces chief witch Mother Demdike into a set of characters hitherto dominated by the witches of 1634. It is not clear why she should suddenly return to prominence at this time. Certainly from this period onwards, Mother Demdike took precedence as the archetypal chief witch in all theatrical performances. The play itself was in almost continual production at Drury Lane from 1702 to 1729, and the name of one of the eighteenth-century actresses appearing in the piece has come down to us. This was Susannah Cox, whose favourite role in any play was that of Theodosia in *The Lancashire Witches*, which she first acted on 4th September 1708.[12]

It has been said that witches were so popular that Restoration theatre-goers could not conceive of an opera without them. Shadwell's play, along with others of its type, must have owed much of its popularity to the special effects employed to

THEATRE-ROYAL, MANCHESTER.

This prefent Evening, MONDAY, *October* 16, 1780.

Will be prefented a favourite COMEDY, call'd,

The RIVALS.

(Written by R. B. SHERIDAN, Efq; Author of The School for Scandal, Duenna, &c. &c.)

Sir Antony Abfolute, by Mr. ROBERTSON
Captain Abfolute, by Mr. KENNEDY
Sir Lucius O'Trigger, by Mr. WILLIAMSON
Acres, by Mr. CONNOR
Davy, by Mr. HOLLINGSWORTH
Fag, by Mr. PALMER
Coachman, by Mr. BANKS——Boy, by Mafter WILSON
And Faulkland, by Mr. WARD

Lydia Languifh, by Mrs. KNIVETON
Mrs. Malaprop, by Mrs. SYMONS
Lucy, by Mifs DILLON——Maid, by Mrs. TANNETT
And Julia, by Mrs. KENNEDY

To which will be added, (for the laft Time, during the Company's prefent ftay) the
laft NEW PANTOMIME ENTERTAINMENT, called,

The Lancafhire Witches;

Or, HARLEQUIN Every Where.

Harlequin, by Mr. BANKS
Pantaloon, by Mr. BATES——Scotchman, by Mr. PALMER
And the Clown, by Mr. HOLLINGSWORTH
The Lancafhire Witches, by Mr. TANNETT, Mrs. SYMONS, Mifs DILLON,
Mrs. PALMER, &c. &c.
And Colombine, by Mrs. TANNETT

The MUSIC compofed by Mr. *Wainwright* —The SCENERY painted by Mr. *Banks.*

In which are feveral VIEWS in this COUNTY, particularly,

The DOCK GATES, at LIVERPOOL.

THE

EXCHANGE, BULL's-HEAD, and INFIRMARY, at MANCHESTER.

With ADDITIONAL MACHINERY.

And a NEW SCENE, reprefenting

A VIEW of ARDWICK-GREEN.

The Whole to conclude with a RURAL DANCE.

Theatre Royal playbill (1780) naming Mr and Mrs Tannett
(Courtesy of Manchester Central Library Theatre Collection)

bring the witches' supernatural frolics to life, which became ever more elaborate as the years passed. 1672–3, for example, saw a new production of Davenant's *Macbeth*, which had audiences gasping as the three witches flew in over the pit on their broomsticks, and Hecate descended onto the stage in a chariot decorated with devils and scenes of hell. An advert for Shadwell's play dated 27th May 1721 in the *Weekly Packet*, tells us that the performance would employ 'all the original Decorations of Rising, Sinking and Flying'. No doubt the actors playing Mother Demdike and her cronies – like *Macbeth*'s witches – put on quite an aerial aerobatics display which must have looked most spectacular.[13]

While often described as a runaway success, Shadwell's play did not receive universal acclamation, as demonstrated by a letter written by a male eighteenth-century incarnation of Mary Whitehouse – published on 11th August 1711 in *The Spectator*. The gentleman indignantly described the play as a 'rabble of broomsticks', by which he was 'haunted for above three hours', and he could not find the subject of sacrifice of black lambs to the Devil any fit subject for humour. Comparing the role played by Shadwell's witches with those in *Macbeth* he pontificates, 'This [*Macbeth*] therefore is a proper Machine where the Business is dark, horrid and bloody; but is extremely foreign from the Affair of Comedy.' [14] He also found the tone of Shadwell's piece immoral and 'an outrage upon modesty' and it has to be admitted that the play is at times a little bawdy even by today's standards. No doubt his letter saw to it that the queues to see the play lengthened considerably!

The comic role played by the Lancashire witches (and witches in general) on the stage in the seventeenth and early eighteenth century is an interesting one. Belief in the *maleficia* of witches was ostensibly on the decline among the educated classes by the late seventeenth century, eventually leading to the repeal of the Witchcraft Act in 1736. However, many people undoubtedly continued to fear witches and took strenuous measures to protect their persons, their homes and their animals against evil magic. Fear and fascination marched hand in hand. The sophisticated London theatre-goers may well have experienced real anxiety as they watched a play in which grotesque and rustic hags could cause such disorder and were able to bewitch their 'betters'. It is almost as if the comic element in plays and operas sought to disempower these cackling creatures on broomsticks that haunted the dreams and imaginations of their audience.

Already a familiar and stereotypical 'comedy' character, Mother Demdike finally took the next logical step and evolved into a perhaps even less threatening 'wicked witch' pantomime villain. In 1757, she appeared as a character in a 'Lilliputian pantomime' entitled *Harlequin's Frolic or a voyage to Prussia* at the Haymarket[15] alongside well-known pantomime characters Harlequin, Columbine and Clown. By this period, the image of the stereotypical witch wearing a pointed hat and seated upon a broom had probably been fixed for some time. Indeed it is very possible that this familiar image evolved from traditional stage costumes worn by witches in theatrical productions in the seventeenth and eighteenth centuries, in order to make them instantly recognisable characters to the audience. The pointed hat may have originally been chosen by the costume designers because it resembled fairy headgear, or even simply because it was very similar to that worn by country folk in the seventeenth century.

Certainly late eighteenth-century woodcuts such as one illustrating the pamphlet *The Famous History of the Lancashire Witches*,[16] thought to date from about 1780, depicts a witch in traditional pointed hat and seated upon a broom-stick; this publication was probably a tribute to their popularity on the stage by this time. On Monday 16th October of the same year, a new pantomime entitled *The Lancashire Witches or, Harlequin Every Where* was in production at the Theatre Royale in Manchester. A playbill has survived for this performance which featured a well-known husband and wife acting duo, Mr and Mrs Tannett.[17]

Over the coming years, Mother Demdike and the Lancashire witches were to become increasingly popular characters in pantomime and other public enter-tainments. In December 1783, a major new pantomime called *The Lancashire Witches and the Distresses of Harlequin* opened at the Royal Circus theatre in London.[18] The music was written by Charles Dibden (the theatre manager) and the songs are still extant.[19] The pantomime was written and conceived by Giuseppe Grimaldi, father of the world-famous clown Joseph Grimaldi, after whom all clowns are known as 'Joey'. Joseph Grimaldi made his first appearance as an infant dancer in 1781 and it is quite possible, therefore, that the greatest character in English pantomime appeared as a child alongside Mother Demdike in his father's production.

By the late eighteenth century, Lancashire witches, as well as being stock pantomime characters, had, in a rather bizarre twist, come to be used as an epithet to refer to the beautiful ladies of Lancashire. The county had long held a reputation for the beauty of its women, and as early as 1622 William Drayton

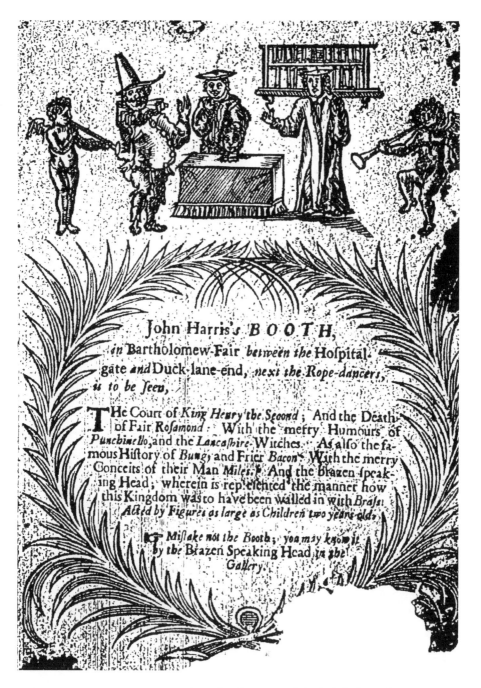

The earliest known English playbill, dating from circa 1655
(Reproduced courtesy of Harvard Theatre Collection)

commented in his vast poem *Poly-Olbion*: 'Old Cheshire is well known to be the 'chief of men'/Fair women doth belong to Lancashire again.' [20] In 1789, it was reported in *World* that a dinner had been held in Manchester to celebrate the return to sanity of George III. In the toasts offered after the banquet, a toast to the Lancashire witches immediately followed the toast to His Majesty, the Queen and the Royal Family, and took precedence over The Lord Chancellor and other political figures.[21] Already very popular characters, the Lancashire witches were to gain iconic status when the nineteenth century fell completely in love with them in their dual guise of hideous hag and charming enchantress.

The Legendary Lancashire Witches

Events in the academic world were about to ensure that the popularity of the Lancashire witches shot into the stratosphere. In 1845 the Chetham Society republished Thomas Potts' *The Wonderful Discoverie of Witchcraft in the Countie of Lancaster*. Potts' work had actually been mentioned in 1780, in a book called *British Topography*, and had even appeared in print some years earlier, when Sir Walter Scott published it in the Somers Tracts.[22]

Nineteenth-century illustration depicting the dual perception of the Lancashire witch as both hideous, scary hag, and charming temptress

However, it was the fact that James Crossley of the Chetham Society was a great friend of a major novelist which ensured the future legendary status of the Lancashire witches. Harrison Ainsworth[23] was so inspired by the 1612 case when it was brought to his attention by Crossley that he decided to write a novel starring Mother Demdike, Mother Chattox and their respective broods (with a guest appearance by Thomas Potts himself). Published initially in serial form in *The Sunday Times* in 1848, the novel was published in book form in 1849, with an illustrated edition coming out in 1854. The book has never been out of print since.

The Lancashire Witches: A Romance of Pendle Forest is a magnificent Gothic romance in which the witches were firmly established as characters left over from some fictitious 'Merrie England'. Thanks to Ainsworth, not just Demdike, but also Alizon and the other the witches of 1612, now took centre stage, a position from which they have never been dislodged. These were now *the* Lancashire witches and the witches involved in the 1634 case (who had appeared alongside

Demdike in earlier plays, pantomimes and ballads and kept interest in Lancashire witchcraft green) were completely upstaged and ended up more or less forgotten.

In the wake of Ainsworth's novel, the witches cast ever more powerful spells on the imaginations of their adoring public. Although a new play, *The Witch Wife: A Tale of Malkin Tower*, by Henry Spicer, failed to capture public imagination at the Marylebone Theatre in 1849,[24] the witches continued to appear as successful guest characters in pantomime in London and northern theatre. Demdike and company joined Tim Bobbin,[25] the Lancashire dialect writer, as characters in the 1851 production of *Harlequin and Tim Bobbin or: The Lancashire Witches* at the Theatre Royal in Liverpool. To give a little flavour of a pantomime of the time, it is interesting to see how a nineteenth-century performance opened:

> The first scene presented to the audience is the village of Milnrow, near Rochdale and Tim Bobbin's Cottage, by moonlight. As the curtain slowly rises a number of Lancashire witches are seen in the distance, performing certain aerial gyrations, each mounted on a broomstick. Shortly afterwards they descend to terra firma, when Mother Demdike, the principal amongst the workers of evil, calls upon her dependents to render their assistance in punishing their most deadly foe, Tim Bobbin.[26]

The witches continued to appear as characters in pantomime for the rest of the century. Indeed, it seemed that no show was complete without Mother Demdike and her crew, who appeared in the oddest-sounding productions. In 1864, for example, a performance of *St George and St Patrick or Harlequin, the Lancashire Witches and the Leprechauns* was mentioned,[27] while 1893 saw the Rotunda Theatre in Liverpool produce a pantomime with the title of *Jack and Jill, or The Lancashire Witches and Mother Goose*.[28] It is, however, difficult to beat another Liverpool pantomime of 1866 which rejoiced in the startling name of *Harlequin, Dicky Sam*[29] *and the Liverpool Liver or Oliver Cromwell, Prince Rupert, the Lancashire Witches and their Fairy Army of Mannikins*.[30]

Lancashire witches also appeared in other types of entertainment as well as pantomime. In 1858 they featured in a 'Fairy Extravaganza' at the Royal Lyceum theatre in London. These performances took the form of comic dramas featuring music, topical satire and extremely elaborate stage effects; they were considered far more elegant and refined than the vulgar entertainment provided by pantomime. In the same year, the Lancashire witches featured in a 'ballet of broomsticks' at the same theatre.[31] An 'equestrian spectacle' (a sort of play enacted by horses and riders) featuring the witches and written by one Tom Fillis was in production in

A typical nineteenth-century Lancashire witch – pretty as a picture. (Illustration from Henry Spicer's 'The Witch Wife, A Tale of Malkin Tower', 1849)

1876,[32] and in 1879 they appeared in their very own comic opera at the Theatre Royal in Manchester. Entitled *The Lancashire Witches or King James' Frolic*, the three-act opera was written by R. T. Gunton, who for some reason best known to himself inveigled Matthew Hopkins, the East Anglian Witchfinder General, into the company of Alizon Device et al. The music for the opera was written by F. Stanislaus.[33]

Nineteenth-century musicians and songwriters also got in on the act by featuring the celebrated sorceresses in their work. New music for 1853 dedicated to them included *The Lancashire Witches Schottische*, composed by Albert Schwitzer, and a *Lancashire Witch Polka*, composed by J. E. Perring,[34] followed by a new waltz in 1870[35] and *The Lancashire Witches Gallop for the Pianoforte* by Thomas Simpson in 1873. Also written at some time, probably in the mid-nineteenth century, is a song *The Lancashire Witches*, whose words have been preserved. This may have been the same song composed by a gentleman called J. B. Geoghegan who died in 1889 and whose obituary mentions that he was the composer of the well-known songs *John Barleycorn* and *The Lancashire Witches*.[36]

'A Lancashire Witch', by William Bradley c. 1913 (Reproduced by kind permission of Salford Art gallery)

In 1869, no less a personage than Charles Dickens paid homage to the charms of the fair women of Lancashire in their role as 'Lancashire witches'. On Saturday 10th April in that year, Liverpool hosted a grand banquet in St George's Hall in honour of the famous writer, complete with a silver fountain spouting rose water and with 700 invited guests and 500 spectators. At the end of the banquet, Dickens arose to propose the toast to 'The Ladies':

> Gentlemen, for I address myself solely to you, for the nature of the toast I am about to propose cannot, I think, be better or more briefly expressed than in a short quotation, from Shakespeare, slightly altered:- Scene, a banqueting hall; thunder of admiration! lightning of eyes! – Enter Macbeth: 'Who are these, so sparkling and so bright in their attire that they look not like inhabitants of earth, and yet are of it? (Laughter.) Reply: Sir, these are the Lancashire witches'. (Loud laughter.)[37]

In the late eighteenth century and during most of the nineteenth, the beautiful ladies of Lancashire had become completely accustomed to hearing themselves referred to collectively as Lancashire witches. The only significant painting of a Lancashire witch from this period I have been able to track down seems to portray this idea of a beautiful lady of the county rather than anything resembling a crone. By William Bradley (1801–1857), the painting entitled *A Lancashire Witch* (c.1838) portrays a pretty young girl sitting in a wood, wearing a hat over her ringlets.[38] In 1867 the *Gentleman's Magazine* commented, 'Hers is a merry face; just such a face as can make glad the hearts of many, and yet be content to throw a spell over only one.' [39] By this period, the witch, as well as being a grotesque comedy stereotype, was also paradoxically seen as a romantic heroine, using her arts and spells merely to make herself irresistible to the opposite sex. In both cases, the image of a Lancashire witch as a strong and independent female capable of wielding negative magical power had been well and truly crushed. Only in remote country villages did people still truly fear the witch and continue to protect themselves against her *maleficia*.

What's in a Name?

Well on her way to becoming a 'brand', 'Lancashire Witch' thus became a snappy, attractive and appropriate choice to name anything from a train to a ship or a racehorse. Few people are aware, for example, that the forerunner of Robert Stephenson's famous locomotive, *The Rocket*, was called *The Lancashire Witch*. Built by Robert Stephenson and Company in 1828, she was a 0-4-0 locomotive weighing 7 tons and capable of pulling an impressive load of 40 tons. She was built at Newcastle-upon-Tyne and was used on both the Bolton and Leigh, and the Liverpool and Manchester Railways.[40] Curiously, on 24th December 1984, Funafuti-Tuvalu (a Polynesian island nation) issued two very attractive stamps which featured Stephenson's *Lancashire Witch*.

The Pendle Witch Locomotive at Clitheroe Station (Photo: Colin Carr)

Later locomotives have been named after the witches over the years, including a narrow gauge engine in 1876,[41] and the London, Midland and Scottish Railway Royal Scot Class 4-6-0 locomotive, number 6125, which was built in Glasgow in 1927. A Class 86 locomotive 86 213 that was named *Lancashire Witch* on 13th March 1981 at Burnley, was preserved in operational condition by the AC Locomotive group.[42] In the last few years it has been possible to take a trip on a steam train that has been named Pendle Witch especially for the excursion.

'Lancashire Witch' was also a very popular name for ships. As early as 1741, a sloop with this name was captured by Spanish pirates near Barbados.[43] In 1761 another *Lancashire Witch*, a 120 ton snow (pronounced snoo, a type of brig normally used by merchants) commanded by Charles Ratcliffe was advertised 'for sale by the candle' at Lloyd's Coffee House, Lombard St, London by John Hutchinson, Broker.[44] This was a type of auction where half an inch of candle was lit and the person who made a bid as the candle flame sputtered out was declared the winner.

In 1771 a ship called the *Lancashire Witch*, sailing from Liverpool, was engaged in the African slave trade.[45] At this period, about a hundred ships a year left Liverpool for Africa. A typical slaving ship would have been armed with 16 guns and could be recognised by the ventilation ports constructed below deck, where the slaves were confined in disgusting conditions and secured by leg irons. The prisoners sometimes brought charms, or 'fetishes', from home on board ship. The diary of slave trader John Newton (who later wrote the hymn *Amazing Grace* when he had 'seen the light') describes how on board his ship, the slaves attempted to use their charms to effect the deaths of the ship's crew by putting these artefacts in the drinking water. Sadly, their *'maleficia'* was discovered.[46]

Another *Lancashire Witch* was a clipper ship chartered by Shaw, Savill & Company to carry 420 immigrants from Liverpool to Lyttleton in New Zealand in 1863. Commanded by Captain West, she was a full-rigged ship of 1574 tons and was painted by celebrated marine artist Thomas Dutton (1819–1891). According to a diary kept by one of the passengers, Henry Thorne Shepherd, this seems to have been a trying voyage for all concerned. His entry for 28th August records, 'We have seen a great number of sea birds of different sorts. One called the Albertross [sic], something like a goose but their wings are longer. One was caught by hook and line.' [47] The albatross is a bird enshrouded in a mass of superstition as it is thought to possess the soul of a dead sailor. One thing you certainly shouldn't do on board any ship is catch one. To kill an albatross was seafaring taboo, invariably leading to disaster as Coleridge famously described in his 1798 poem *The Rime of the Ancient Mariner*:

> God save thee, ancient Mariner,
> From the fiends that plague thee thus! —
> Why look'st thou so?' — 'With my crossbow
> I shot the Albatross.

> And I had done a hellish thing,
> And it would work 'em woe:
> For all averred, I had killed the bird
> That made the breeze to blow.
> Ah wretch! said they, the bird to slay,
> That made the breeze to blow!

And strike disaster it did, though not in the shape of a storm. Instead, scarlet fever broke out on board *the Lancashire Witch*, along with whooping cough and measles. In the three months or so at sea, 3 adults and 23 children lost their lives.

Apart from a cruise ship bearing the name in 1881, aboard which nothing untoward seems to have happened, the name 'Lancashire Witch' does not seem to have been a particularly lucky one in maritime history. On Christmas Day 1903, the SS *Coogee* whose original name back in 1888 was *Lancashire Witch*, collided with a sailing ship in thick fog on its way to Melbourne, killing its captain. Having been refitted, the ship continued to be involved in accidents. Its owners eventually blasted the craft with explosives until it sank in 1928. Lying in 105 feet of water, the picturesque wreck is now a favourite haunt of divers in what is known as 'the ships' graveyard' at Port Phillip Heads, just south of Melbourne in Victoria.[48]

Having bewitched the nineteenth century in her dual roles of enchanting temptress and hideous pantomime hag, the Lancashire witch showed no inclination to relinquish her hold on the imagination of the public, as the century drew to a close. With improved communications and the arrival of television, the twentieth century offered fresh opportunities to promote Pendle, the Ribble Valley and Lancaster as tourist destinations where eager visitors could immerse themselves in the legend of the famous witches of Lancashire.

CHAPTER SEVEN

The Wonderful Witches of Lancashire

'Hear now the words of the witches,
The secrets we bid in the night,
When dark was our destiny's pathway,
That now we bring forth into light.' [1]

n the early twentieth century, staging historical spectacles and pageants became a very popular pastime, especially among the middle classes. With history itself being regarded as a kind of progression, each episode in a pageant was intended to illustrate to its spectators how the world was 'getting better'.[2] By this time, it would have been unthinkable for Lancastrians to organise an event such as this without paying homage to the witches who were now celebrated characters in the history of Lancashire. No public show was considered complete without them.

One of these typical pre-war pageants was staged in Lancaster in 1913. The Town Hall was temporarily renamed 'Pageant hall', and bustled with activity as many willing hands designed and sewed together the hundreds of costumes needed for residents taking part in the spectacle. One of the most elaborate episodes re-enacted in Springfield Park was the trial of the Lancashire witches, with a script written by the novelist Halliwell Sutcliffe who specialised in romantic historical fiction.[3] Photographs of the event suggest that great care was taken with the witches' costumes and it is noticeable that there isn't a pointed hat in sight!

To mark the occasion, a set of six illustrations depicting scenes from Lancaster's history was produced. One of these was a watercolour painting entitled *Trial of Witches, 1612* by artist Fred Kirk Shaw (shown on page 14), which is now held in the collections of Lancaster City and Maritime Museum.[4]

Two views of the Lancaster pageant in Springfield Park, 1913

The 1935 Clitheroe pageant

The Rolls Royce jet-propelled witches, Clitheroe torchlight procession, 1948

In May 1935, Clitheroe staged a pageant illustrating the town's history through the ages. The witches were portrayed in all their pointy-hatted glory by the Waterloo Wesley Scholars, whose organiser promised a reporter that the whole episode would conclude with the hanging of a witch. The reporter expressed deep disappointment when the promised execution failed to materialise on the day.[5] In 1948 the town again produced an elaborate historical entertainment to celebrate the 800th anniversary of the granting of the town's charter. A pageant held against the picturesque backdrop of Clitheroe Castle included *The Strange and Terrible Story of a Trial in which Evil is Illustrated, Portrayed and Punished*. The witches on trial were again portrayed by a church group,[6] this time members of Waterloo Methodist Chapel.

On this occasion, Clitheroe also staged one of its traditional torchlight processions. The theme of one float was Rolls Royce's 'jet propelled witches', decorated with a drawing of a witch flying upon a jet plane rather than a broomstick.[7] This was a tribute to the fact that the Rolls Royce company was at that time involved in the development of Sir Frank Whittle's jet engine at nearby Barnoldswick. It was also an acknowledgement of Whittle's many connections with Clitheroe.

The Father of Modern Witchcraft

At around the same time that Clitheroe was celebrating its 'jet propelled witches', a man was living in Liverpool, to whom merely dressing up as a witch wasn't particularly satisfying, because he believed himself to be the genuine article. Dr Gerald Gardner – known today as the 'father of modern witchcraft' – was born at The Glen, Blundellsands, in 1884. He developed his new witchcraft beliefs in association with other friends in the occult world including Cecil Williamson and the celebrated high magician Aleistair Crowley (affectionately known as 'the Great Beast'!). It is therefore true to say that not only was Lancashire the scene of the most famous witch trial in history, but it was also the birthplace of a *bona fide*, brand new witchcraft religion called Wicca, which now boasts many thousands of adherents.

Gardner claimed to have been initiated into an underground coven of witches (led by someone called 'Old Dorothy'), that was directly descended from one of the ancient covens, most of which were, according to Dr Margaret Murray, pagan cults driven underground by Christianity.[8] In 1954, he published *Witchcraft Today* and this book was instrumental in the development of modern witchcraft. Many of today's covens still follow the 'Gardnerian' tradition.[9]

Gerald Gardner and Lois Bourne sailing in Greece in 1962
(Photograph courtesy of Lois Bourne)

In his book *The Possessed*, Brian McConnell alleges that my late friend and mentor, Ralph Merrifield of the Museum of London, was once seen by Gerald Gardner as a potential recruit to the witch cult. Gardner apparently invited Ralph to a meeting where he said there would be dances. Asked what sort of dances, Gardner said, 'Fox trots and other ballroom dances.' Seeing the disappointment on Merrifield's face, he hastily added, 'Of course, we take all our clothes off first!' According to McConnell, Ralph declined the invitation.

I remember Ralph telling me that when he was in Ghana, his doorbell rang one stormy night and he opened the door to find Gerald Gardner grinning on his doorstep, hair and beard flowing wildly in the wind, wanting to have a discussion about witchcraft. Ralph didn't mention the dancing episode to me, but I would imagine he would have enjoyed all these encounters immensely. He regarded Gerald Gardner and his witchcraft theories with his customary amused tolerance and benevolent interest.

There have been numerous attempts in recent years to play down both Dr Gardner's reliability and his contribution to the formation of the religion of

Wicca. It is certainly likely that, with friends, he invented many of the rituals he claimed to have learned from a secret circle of witches, and there seems to be no doubt that he was a bit of a voyeur. But however and whenever it was founded, thanks to Gerald Gardner and his followers, the Craft is now a thriving pagan religion with many thousands of adherents both here and abroad. Nobody can realistically refute Gardner's role in the great pagan witchcraft revival of the twentieth century and I regret that I never made his acquaintance.

Born in a town near Preston, Lois Bourne is another famous and influential modern Lancashire witch. A prolific writer on the subject of witchcraft,[10] she was initiated by Gerald Gardner himself and became High Priestess of the Bricket Wood coven in the 1960s. Lois, who has lived in St Albans for many years, has often advised researchers on the Lancashire witch case[11] and has loaned various magical items for witchcraft exhibitions in the county. Several years ago I happened to mention to her that my favourite fictional witch character was Celia in Robert Neill's novel *Witchfire at Lammas*. Delighted, Lois exclaimed, 'That's ME!' It turned out that Robert Neill had consulted her about the book and had been so impressed that he based his main character upon her.

Lois has a refreshing and outspoken attitude to today's magical practitioners. She has nothing but contempt for many modern witches and covens, regarding them as phonies with leaders who are 'the blind leading the blind'. If they all congregated together, Lois opines, they wouldn't even be able to summon up the power to boil a cauldron of water![12]

Her attitude to the witches of 1612 is also interesting. She does not regard them as 'real witches' with 'real power'. It is certainly the case that modern witches seem to have very little in common with historical witches, whose religious background was very firmly Christian, rather than pagan. However, I think few historians would argue with the idea that many historical witches such as Demdike and Chattox seem to have had a very firm belief in their own occult powers, and that many of their spells and charms would often have 'worked' very much in the same way as a modern Wiccan's – that is, through the application of psychology.[13] If you think a witch is casting a spell to help you with an illness, for example, the psychological benefits of this knowledge will often make you better before the witch has had time to lift a finger! Equally, if you think a witch has it in for you, worrying about it could very easily make you ill. To be able to inspire faith (or fear) and work magic in this particular way requires an extremely powerful and charismatic personality such as that possessed by Lois Bourne, and probably possessed also by Demdike and Chattox.

A Silly Lancashire Witch

These days, modern witches follow a variety of different traditions. One offshoot of the Gardnerian form of Wicca is the Alexandrian tradition. This was named originally after another modern 'witch' called Alex Sanders, who also hailed from Lancashire. Born in 1926 in Birkenhead, his family moved to Manchester soon after his birth. Sanders worked for a time at the John Ryland's Library, because an angel apparently told him to apply for a job there. Together with his very pretty wife Maxine, he certainly raised the profile of modern witchcraft, but not in any good way. His 'magic' generally seemed to involve people writhing point-lessly around in the nude and having people take photographs of the shenanigans. Rather than any sort of magical ceremony, it looks like ... well, it looks like a lot of people writhing pointlessly about in the nude! *Legend of the Witches*, a film documenting the history of witchcraft, contained a lot of this pointless nude writhing. Starring Sanders and his wife, it came out in 1970. Few cinemas showed it.

Alex Sanders claimed to be in contact with a very interesting familiar spirit that spoke through him (Sanders calls it channelling). This familiar called himself

Looking across the River Calder towards Whalley Abbey

Nick Demdike. Speaking in a broad Lancashire accent he claimed to be one of the witches executed in 1612 and told Sanders and his coven to go to Whalley Abbey where they would find his ancient *athame* (a witch's ritual knife), which he had thrown in a brook in the seventeenth century. According to Mr Demdike (speaking through Sanders), it was at Whalley Abbey that the Lancashire witches used to hatch their plots to overthrow the king and re-establish the monasteries. The coven couldn't get to the brook by the abbey fast enough but were distraught when they arrived to find the brook had turned into a river. (Yes, that would be the River Calder.) Miraculously, they found the knife almost immediately and drove back to Manchester with their 'precious relic'.[14]

Now, it was really very clever indeed of Alex Sanders and his coven to find the *athame* of Nick Demdike, because Nick Demdike never existed. He was a fictional character in Harrison Ainsworth's novel *The Lancashire Witches*. If this is an example of Alex Sanders' credibility then it is perhaps astonishing that we have heard no reports of converts being persuaded to worship entities such as the Great Bell-Capped Witch-God Noddy and his demonic sidekick Big Ears. Luckily for more serious practitioners of the craft, Wicca managed to survive this self-delusional posturing.

This confusion between fictional events described by novelists and the actual events of 1612 continues to cause problems today. There are still, for example, people who seem to believe that the Lancashire witches held midnight Sabbats at Whalley Abbey in spite of the fact that this incident is also a fictional event in Harrison Ainsworth's marvellous book.

A great deal more accurate and down to earth than Ainsworth's Gothic novel was Manchester-born writer Robert Neill's treatment of the story, *Mist over Pendle*.[15] First published in 1951, Neill produced a cracking good read, which was at the same time accessible to the general reader and meticulously well researched and well written. The author, who was at that time living in Cumberland, was the

A still from the 1976 BBC production of 'The Witches of Pendle'
(Photo reproduced courtesy of the Burnley Express)

guest of honour at a major witchcraft exhibition staged by Towneley Hall in the summer of 1972; this ambitious project attracted over 90,000 visitors.[16]

Since Robert Neill's *Mist over Pendle* appeared, novels that re-imagine the witches' story continue to be churned out regularly, but few can claim similar quality to those of Ainsworth and Neill. The witches have also made occasional guest appearances – thinly disguised – in other major novels. Terry Pratchett's Lancre witches seem to nod acknowledgement to our witches, and in *Good Omens*, the characters Anathema Device and Agnes Nutter even bear the same surnames as a couple of the Lancashire witches. It is amusing to note that Pratchett and Gaiman's witchfinder, Shadwell, is also the name of the writer of the play *The Witches of Lancashire*, whom we have had cause to mention on several occasions. The Lancashire witches also appear as characters in the popular Spook novels of Joseph Delaney.

Television, Theatre and Music

On 16th June 1976 the BBC broadcast a television drama featuring the Lancashire witches.[17] *The Witches of Pendle* was a high quality, if very dark, production, capturing perfectly the brooding Pendle locations and the deprived and uncivilised conditions in which the witch families struggled to survive. Written by Barry Collins, it starred the excellent Cathryn Harrison as Alizon Device – around whom the whole story revolved – with John Stratton appearing as Roger Nowell. A major (fictional) role was assigned to the pedlar's son Abraham Law, played by James Laurenson, whose character was used to personify the overzealous fanaticism of the rabid witchfinder. A new drama or documentary about the Lancashire witches seems long overdue.

In the late 1980s it felt very briefly as if we were well and truly back in 1612, when an evangelical vicar attempted to drum up support for the erection of a massive 20 metre cross on top of Pendle Hill. He had already persuaded his flock and was trying to persuade others, that the whole area was once more under threat from Lancashire witches and Satanists, and he wanted to reclaim it for Christ.

Kevin Logan, Vicar of St Johns, Great Harwood, was a member of the Evangelical Alliance, a group which at this particular time had a bee (or possibly an enormous hornet) in its bonnet about the existence of an widespread satanic conspiracy.[18] Luckily, he was refused planning permission on the grounds that the cross would constitute a 'new development'! His activities attracted the

Cover design of Symbiosis, an album by Demdike Stare

attention of a BBC film maker Paul Pawlikowski, whose documentary *Lucifer over Lancashire* was broadcast to a bemused audience in 1987.

By far the most unfortunate treatment of the Lancashire witches on television was served up by the *Most Haunted: Live* team in the episodes which became known by their fans as 'Pendle Hell'. Broadcast for Halloween over three nights in October 2004, the night-time antics of Yvette Fielding and Derek Acorah reached a large audience and probably set the image of the Lancashire witches back by at least 400 years. Acorah could not even get the names of the witches right, 'I will never forget the name Anne Shepherd!' he declared melodramatically to nobody in particular. Who? After the break, he began to talk about Anne Redfearn instead.

During the famous séance at Tyndale Farm, when the spirits of the witches attempted to throttle the whole team (but sadly failed), Acorah spat out several times that the witches were 'filthy souls'. He also accused Alizon Device of cutting up bodies, severing fingers and torturing victims – all in all, an absolutely unforgivable travesty of the truth. Even in this day and age, people tend to believe what they see on television and the regrettable outcome of this programme was the dissemination of yet more inaccurate information about the witches.

Luckily this pointless and negative media hype is offset by artists whose creativity is today stimulated by the Lancashire witches in more positive directions. New music bands such as *Demdike Stare* take the witches as their inspiration, for example, while one musician even named herself after a

Lancashire witch. This is Alice Nutter, former member of the band Chumbawamba who is from Burnley and so grew up in the shadow of Pendle Hill, immersed in the witch lore. Alice is now an active film, television and theatrical writer. Having cut her teeth on such shows as *Casualty* and *The Street*, she has recently written a play about the Lancashire witches called *The Power*, which is an inventive blending of factual and fictional characters.[19]

Other playwrights continue to produce interesting versions of the story. In contrast to the Restoration 'machine plays' and nineteenth-century pantomime extravaganzas – when spectacle was everything – recent plays such as *Cold Light Singing* and the very successful theatrical production *Sabbat*, take a more intimate and thought-provoking look at the events of 1612.

Indeed, artists of all disciplines are increasingly using the story as a creative springboard to create eclectic works of art which utilise themes suggested by the Lancashire witches. We have already had an exhibition by painter Joe Hesketh at The Dukes, Lancaster, in 2009, while Blake Morrison published a selection of his poems entitled *Pendle Witches* in 1996. Exploring gender and sexuality, the poems were illustrated by celebrated artist Paula Rego. Hopefully the 400th anniversary of the trial and executions in 2012 will stimulate many more innovative treatments and unusual visions of the witches' story.

Casting a Spell on Tourists

The Pendle witches are today an exceptionally valuable resource for Lancashire tourism. Visitors to the county can take a fascinating tour of Lancaster Castle and sample its dark dungeons, or climb Pendle Hill if they are feeling particularly energetic. If they fancy looking for some of the many ghosts who eluded the *Most Haunted* team, they could lie in wait for the spectre of an old witch pushing a wheelbarrow through solid walls in the fields above Rough Lee School.[20] Alternatively they could hang around Jinny Well at Newchurch-in-Pendle where they may very well be hassled by a headless boggart.[21] They could also take a trip either on foot or by car to visit some of the places associated with Demdike, Chattox and their respective broods. A trip to Pendle would not be complete without a trip to the shop *Witches Galore* at Newchurch-in-Pendle, where Maureen has been selling souvenirs, books, t-shirts and occult jewellery for the

Lancaster Castle dungeon

Witches Galore at Newchurch-in-Pendle

past thirty years. After a browse round the shop, a short walk will take the visitor to St Mary's Church where they can examine the all-seeing eye of God, with the added bonus of the so-called grave of Alice Nutter nearby.[22] This tombstone is protected by law as a Grade II listed monument.

Should they feel so inclined, tourists could also take in Pendle Witch Camp run by Adrian Lord for the past seven years. Here they can listen to folk bands, attend talks, workshops and generally have a good time at the Summer Solstice. Anybody that fancies a different sort of experience should visit Hawkshaw Farm Park at Clayton-le-Dale. In 2012, it will be possible to pet farm animals and consume Amanda Dowson's gorgeous ice cream before attempting to find a way through an 8 foot high maize maze in the shape of a Lancashire witch. Amanda will also be hosting an outdoor theatre 'scare attraction' at the farm where just about anything could happen in the maze, including bumping into Mother Demdike herself!

Those with a penchant for a good pint should try one of Moorhouse's Lancashire witch-inspired ales. The brewery is planning a special 'witch poster' to celebrate the witches' anniversary in 2012. Public houses named after the witches can be found at Sabden and Atherton, just outside Manchester.

Witch-spotting residents and visitors could also look out for Transdev's fleet of luxury buses which carry passengers between Nelson and Manchester. Travelling the X43 and X44 Witch Way route, the company has carried on the tradition of naming modes of transport after the witches and it is possible to take a ride on the Anne Whittle, James Device or even on the Judge Bromley if you are feeling a bit anti-witch that particular day!

One thing the visitor will regrettably not be able to find in Pendle, however, is a museum dedicated to our local witches. It is interesting to note that Cecil Williamson – the old friend and enemy of the 'father of modern witchcraft' Gerald Gardner – refused to lend any items from his own occult collection to the Towneley Hall exhibition in 1972. This was because in the 1950s Cecil had originally intended to set up his Museum of Witchcraft in the Pendle area rather than in Cornwall.[23] As he was consistently refused planning permission at this time, he evidently saw no reason to assist anyone attempting to stage a witchcraft exhibition in a place where his own museum had been rejected. Cecil took a positive delight in being quite vindictive when he felt slighted, and on this occasion I find it hard to blame him.

This strange and somewhat snobbish attitude towards a possible museum dedicated to Lancashire witchcraft and magic still lingered well into the 1960s. Edgar Peel and Pat Southern commented in 1969, for example, that 'Pendle

GRAVE ON SOUTH SIDE OF ST. MARY'S CHURCH, NEWCHURCH-IN-PENDLE

The so-called grave of Alice Nutter in the graveyard of Newchurch-in-Pendle

has so far been spared the establishment of any witchcraft museum.' [24] Yet this is precisely what quite a few residents and certainly many visitors today would actually like to see when they visit the area. The huge interest generated by the witches' story at present lacks any real focal point for the visitor. In Salem, Massachusetts, where a famous outbreak of witchcraft took place in 1692, this need is efficiently addressed by the Salem Witch Museum, which informs the visitor about all aspects of the celebrated case.[25] We could do worse than emulate such American ideas in Pendle; one thing the Americans do superbly is entertain and inform their tourists.

Over the past 400 years, the shades of those men and women whose lives were snuffed out on the gallows in Lancaster in August 1612 must have gazed down at their audience in bemused incomprehension. The men had seen themselves largely edited out of the story while the women saw themselves portrayed as anything from satanic hags in league with the Devil to the prank-playing witches of the Jacobean stage. They had even witnessed their own transformation from cackling pantomime crones to the epitome of female Lancashire beauty. Once perceived as the evil plague of Pendle Forest and the terror of all householders and farmers, the Lancashire witches in all their guises are today increasingly celebrated as an immortal symbol representing, for many, the very essence of Lancashire.

> What joy like ours can mortals find?
> We can command the Sea and Wind:
> All Elements our Charms obey,
> And all good things become our prey;
> The daintiest Meat, and lustiest Wine,
> We for our Sabbaths still design.
> 'Mongst all the great Princes the sun shall e'er see,
> None can be so great, or so happy as we.[26]

Endnotes

Endnotes Chapter 1

1   Henry Spicer, *The Witch Wife, A Tale of Malkin Tower*, Song of the Witches, Act III, Scene 2, 1849.
2   The origin of the name Demdike is obscure, and whether her friends and family ever referred to her by this name is unknown.
3   Many of the events in the Device/Demdike story take place in the vicinity of Newchurch. Also, according to Dr Laycock of Sabden, 'In a survey of Goldshawbooth taken in the year 1828, four fields are described in Saddlers Farm; three fields bear the name Malkin.' (See 'Pendle Forest Witches: A Lecture' by Dr Laycock of Sabden, Clitheroe Community History Collection.)
4   That Malkin Tower was a small dwelling is indicated by 'Iter Lancastrense', a poem written in 1636 by Rev. Richard James of Corpus Christi College, Oxford. James visited the area at this time and described the Demdike home as 'Malkin's Tower, a little cottage where reporte makes caitive witches meete to sweare their homage to ye divell.'
5   Dr John Webster, *The Displaying of Supposed Witchcraft*, 1677, Clitheroe Community History Collection, p. 68 and Thomas Potts, *The Wonderful Discoverie of Witches in the Countie of Lancaster*, 1613, (Carnegie Edition, 2004), p. 24.
6   Thomas Potts, *Discoverie*, p. 67.
7   Richard Catlow, *The Pendle Witches*, 1976, p. 14.
8   It is not at all clear whether or not the Devices and Mother Demdike all lived together at Malkin Tower, or whether 'our firehouse' was actually a separate cottage near to Malkin Tower. At one point James Device indicates that his grandmother's and mother's house were two different buildings. (See Potts, *Discoverie*, p. 25)
9   C. L'Estrange Ewan, *Witchcraft and Demonism*, 1933, p. 140.
10 *The House and Farm Accounts of the Shuttleworths of Gawthorpe Hall*, Chetham Society, 1856, p. 240.
11 There is no evidence to suggest that this house, belonging to James Wilsey (or Wilson) can be identified with Ashlar House in Fence. This idea seems to have arisen out of various misunderstandings over the years.
12 James I, *Daemonologie*, Edinburgh, 1597, pp. 50–1.
13 It is unlikely that any genuine Sabbat ever took place outside the imagination of

witch and inquisitor until witchcraft was reinvented by Gerald Gardner in the early twentieth century. (See Norman Cohn, *Europe's Inner Demons*, 1975, pp. 99–126.)

14 Thomas Potts, *Discoverie*, p. 74.

15 For the full story of Jennet Preston, see Jonathan Lumby, *The Lancashire Witch Craze*, 1995.

16 http://www.lancastercastle.com/html/people/tour.php?id=12

17 In *A Guide To Grand-Jury Men Divided Into Two Bookes: In The First, Is The Authors Best Advice To Them what to doe, before they bring in a billa vera in cases of witchcraft, etc*, 1627 by Richard Bernard, he advises that 'they meet to christen (as they speake) their spirits, and give them names.' However, it is likely that the source of his information was the Lancashire witch trial of 1612.

18 *Newes from Scotland*, 1591, (The Book Tree edition, 2002), pp. 16–17.

19 Thomas Potts, *Discoverie*, p. 117.

20 On the site of the later house built by Thomas Covell in the 1630s, now called The Judges' Lodgings.

21 *A History of Lancaster Castle, with an Account of its Remarkable Prisoners and of many Extraordinary Executions*, 1882, p. 10.

22 Cross Fleury, *Time-Honoured Lancaster: Historic Notes on the Ancient Borough of Lancaster*, 1891, p. 67. We should notice that the Well Tower did not seem to be associated with the witches in the nineteenth century.

23 J. S. Cockburn, *A History of the English Assizes*, 1972, p. 107.

24 Potts, *Discoverie*, pp. 65, 78.

25 James Orchard Hall (ed.), *The Palatine Anthology*, 1850, p. 135.

26 E. Kennerley, *Thomas Covell of Lancaster Esquire*, Local Studies No. 11, Lancaster City Museum, n.d.

27 Lancashire Record Office DDKE/3/87 1632/3

28 E. Axon, *Bygone Lancashire*, 1892, pp. 63–4.

29 Where his body has gone is a bit of a mystery as no bones are associated with the memorial. He is probably buried in a long-forgotten vault in the graveyard.

30 Significantly, perhaps, dedicated to Potts' patron, Thomas, Lord Knyvet, who was responsible for uncovering the Gunpowder Plot of 1605.

31 Christine Goodier, *1612: The Lancashire Witch Trials: A New Guide*, 2011.

32 Who, for instance, was Henry Robinson? According to Edward Fairfax, *Demonologia*, 1622, p. 93, Henry Robinson formerly of Old Laund (Fairfax's neighbour at Swinsty Hall, Little Timble, near Harrogate) 'had a former wife bewitched to death by the witches of Lancashire, as you may read in the book made of those witches, and their actions and executions you may read.' I can find no mention of Henry Robinson's wife in Potts' work. Was she edited out, or is Fairfax referring to a *different* and therefore lost work?

33 For a detailed description of each witch's trial, see Edgar Peel and Pat Southern, *The Trials of the Lancashire Witches*, 1969.

34 J. S. Cockburn and T. Green (Eds.), *Twelve Good Men and True: The Criminal Trial Jury in England 1200–1800*, p. 148.

35 The Crown Hall, in which the witches were tried, was in 1796 converted into the Robing Room and Library.

36 G. Durston, *Witchcraft and Witch Trials: A History of English Witchcraft and its Legal Perspectives*, 2009, p. 390.

37 One wonders where Jennet had been between March and August. It is tempting to think that she was being groomed and coached as a dramatic and surprise star witness by Roger Nowell or one of his staff.

38 She was not the mistress of Rough Lee Hall as novelists would have us believe. (See Gladys Whittaker, *Rough Lee Hall – Fact and Fiction*, 1980.)

39 Unless they had murdered their husbands by witchcraft, which was known as *'petit treason'*.

40 Jennet Preston had already been tried and executed at York on 29th July (Gisburn then being in Yorkshire).

41 He was involved in the trial of the Samlesbury witches, tried at the same time as the Pendle witches.

42 The original workhouse lay near the White Cross, an actual cross in the road in the south of the town.

43 *The Lancaster Martyrs*, Incorporated Catholic Truth Society, p. 2.

44 *A History of Lancaster Castle*, 1882, pp. 29–30.

45 G.Durston, *Witchcraft and Witch Trials*, p. 430.

46 Thomas Potts, *Discoverie*, p. 131.

47 http://randomsounds.tripod.com/id4.html.

48 *Gentleman's Magazine*, 1772, p. 195.

49 F. Hill, *A Delusion of Satan: The Full Story of the Salem Witch Trials*, 1995, pp. 171–4.

50 Register Transcripts, Lancashire Parish Register Society, Vol. 32: Baptism, Marriage, Burial, 1599–1690.

51 L. Caroe, 'Bones Find Casts Spell on Workers', *Newcastle Evening Chronicle*, 12th January 2008.

52 http://www.chestertourist.com/stmarys.htm.

53 http://www.yeoldesussexpages.com/history/gaols/gaolmain.htm.

Endnotes Chapter 2

1 William Shakespeare, *Macbeth*, Act IV, Scene 1.

2 George Henry Borrow, *Romano Lavo Lil* (Romany Dictionary), 1874.

3 William Self Weeks, *Clitheroe in the Seventeenth Century*, n.d. p. 93.

4 Lancashire Record Office QSB/1/33/16.

5   Thomas Potts, *Discoverie*, p. 20.

6   Christopher Farone, 'What's New in Ancient Roman Magic: Recent Archaeological Discoveries', *Amphora*, Vol. 5: Issue 2, American Philological Society, pp. 6–9.

7   Richard Cavendish, *The Black Arts*, 1977, p. 29. Reginald Scot also offers long and detailed instructions on fashioning wax images in *The Discoverie of Witchcraft*, 1584, Dover Publications, 1972, p. 146.

8   *Newes from Scotland*, 1591, (The Book Tree edition, 2002), p. 27.

9   Thomas Potts, *Discoverie*, p. 109.

10 Ibid. pp. 110–11.

11 Ibid. pp. 46–7.

12 Ibid. p. 56.

13 Ibid. p. 44.

14 John Aubrey, *Remaines*, (quoted in Iona Opie and Mona Tatem (eds.), *A Dictionary of Superstitions*, 1989, p. 60).

15 And it was, of course, forbidden by law according to the Witchcraft Act of 1604 which specified that no person must *'take up any dead man, woman or child out of his her or their grave ... or the skin, bone or any other part of any dead person, to be employed, or used in any manner of witchcraft, enchantment, charm or sorcery ...'*

16 James I, *Daemonologie*, p. 45.

17 James McKay, *Pendle Hill in History and Literature*, 1888, p. 353.

18 Historical Society of Lancashire & Cheshire, Liverpool, Proceedings and Papers, Vol. 18, 1900, p. 21.

19 William Harrison Ainsworth, *The Lancashire Witches: A Romance of Pendle Forest*, (2006 reprint of Routledge 1884 edition), p. 6.

20 W. Henderson, *Notes on the Folklore of the Northern Counties of England and the Borders*, 1879, pp. 221–4.

21 C. H. Byrne, *The Cross and the Cauldron: A Witches' Book of Lore, Spells and Charms*, 1986, p. 33.

22 J. B. Lang, 'Charming of Cattle', Proceedings of the Dorset Natural History & Archaeological Society 91, 1969, pp. 222–3.

23 J. Harland and T.T. Wilkinson, *Lancashire Witchcraft, Charms and Spells* (originally published as Lancashire Folklore, 1882), p. 2.

24 Quoted in Iona Opie and Mona Tatem (eds), *A Dictionary of Superstitions*, 1989, pp. 203–4.

25 Ibid. p. 202.

26 In a recent cold snap in December 2010, the river at Brungerley froze over. It was reported in the *Daily Mail* and the *Clitheroe Advertiser and Times* (9th December 2010) that a dog had fallen through the ice, closely followed by its owner who was attempting to rescue the animal. The lady concerned was fortunate enough to be saved from an icy death by a passer-by, and the dog saved itself and strolled off as

if nothing had happened. We can imagine Peg lurking in the depths of the river, presumably thinking it was her lucky day, shouting 'Doh!' as both potential sacrifices escaped her.

27 J. Simpson, and S. Roud, *Oxford Dictionary of English Folklore*, 2003, p. 117.

28 James I, *Daemonologie*, pp. 73–4.

29 Robert Kirk, *The Secret Commonwealth of Elves, Fauns and Fairies*, 1691, New York Review Books, 2007, p. 13.

30 Cheshire and Chester Archives & Local Studies Service, Manchester 7, n.d., accessed on A2A.

31 Thomas Potts, *Discoverie*, pp. 39–40.

32 For a full discussion of the links between British fairy beliefs and witch beliefs, see Emma Wilby, *Cunning Folk and Familiar Spirits: Shamanistic Visionary Traditions in Early Modern British Witchcraft and Magic*, 2005.

33 Thomas Potts, *Discoverie*, p. 35.

34 Ibid. pp. 21–2.

35 Nicolas Remy, *Demonolatry: An account of the Historical Practice of Witchcraft*, book 1: chap. XIV, Dover Publications, 2008, p. 57.

36 Thomas Potts, *Discoverie*, p. 22. If the familiars could change their shapes, I suppose there is no reason why they should not take on female form should they feel so inclined.

37 Ibid. pp. 67–8. It is interesting to note that in the 1634 Lancashire witch case, the men do not seem to have been examined for witch marks.

38 Ibid. pp. 68–9.

39 *The Court Rolls of the Honour of Clitheroe in the County of Lancaster*, Vol. II, 1912, p. 132.

40 http://www.instarch.is/instarch/midlun/netverkefni/arena/gogn/hofstadir/

41 Thomas Potts, *Discoverie*, p. 47.

42 Ibid. p. 23.

43 According to John Swain, a cow at this time was worth three pounds or about thirty weeks' net wages for a slater. He also suggests that the cow which Nutter asked Demdike to heal may have been the same one supposedly bewitched by Chattox. (See J. Swain, 'Witchcraft, Economy and Society', *The Lancashire Witches: Histories and Stories*, 2002, p. 75.

44 S. Hickey, 'Fatal Feeds?: Livestock losses and Witchcraft Accusations in Tudor and Stuart Britain', *Folklore*, Vol. 101: ii, 1990 , pp. 133–7.

45 Another well on Pendle Hill, which was apparently marked by a cross in medieval times, is now known as Robin Hood's Well but is likely to have been dedicated originally to Robin Goodfellow. It is also sometimes called Fox's Well, as George Fox – founder of the Quaker movement – drank from it.

46 *The Mad Pranks and Merrie Jests of Robin Goodfellow* (reprinted for the Percy Society from the edition of 1628), 1841.

47 J. Harland and T. T. Wilkinson, *Lancashire Legends, Traditions, Pageants, Sports etc.*, 1873, p. 235.

48 Robert Herrick, *Hesperides*, 1648.

Endnotes Chapter 3

1 Traditional witch's lament (quoted in Mary Nattrass, 'Witch Posts and Early Dwellings in Cleveland', *Yorkshire Archaeological Journal*, 1956).

2 Mary Nattrass, 'Witch Posts', *Gwerin*, Vol. 3, 1962, p. 260.

3 Ibid. p. 255.

4 These were usually small silver brooches in the shape of a heart, placed within children's clothes to protect them from witchcraft and enchantment. Occasionally the heart brooch was fashioned out of 'cold iron'.

5 As illustrated by two eighteenth-century apple corers in the collection of Clitheroe Castle Museum. One bears a heart design and the other something similar to a saltire cross.

6 J. Logan, *The Prediction Book of Amulets and Talismans*, 1986, p. 14.

7 Published in Mary Nattrass, *Gwerin*, Vol. 3, 1962, p. 265. This drawing shows a date of 1691 on the post, which should, it now seems, read 1695.

8 J. B. Taylor, 'The Witchposts of Rossendale', *Valley Magazine*, Rawtenstall Community History Collection, June 1988, p. 48.

9 'The Wood of Thor was a Guard against Witches', *Burnley Evening Star*, Rawtenstall Community History Collection, 12th June 1972.

10 J. B. Taylor, 'The Witchposts of Rossendale', p. 48.

11 'Rawtenstall House with a Witchpost', *Rossendale Free Press*, Rawtenstall Community History Collection, 22nd July 1967.

12 In some parts of India, where this practice still takes place, the designs are called *kolam* patterns. Here they are traced in rice flour on the step and represent an offering to Lakshmi, the goddess of rice, earth and wealth. Lakshmi will then prevent evil spirits from entering the building.

13 Clifford H. Byrne, *Newchurch-in-Pendle: Folklore, Fact and Fiction*, 1982, p. 13. See also the illustration in Byrne's *The Cross and the Cauldron*, p. 10.

14 Ralph Merrifield, *The Archaeology of Ritual and Magic*, p. 129. Another protective device involved the walling up of a cat in the chimney area. We do not seem to have any records of such discoveries in Lancashire at present.

15 Personal communication via email: Rebecca Shawcross, Shoe Resources Officer, Northampton Museums and Art Gallery to Jennie Cobban, 13th December, 2010.

16 Ralph Merrifield, *The Archaeology of Ritual and Magic*, pp. 134–5.

17 N. Webster, *Halls and Manor Houses of North East Lancashire*, 2003, p. 68.

18 Information from George Wolfenden, Fooden Cottage, November 2010.

19 Ralph Merrifield, *The Archaeology of Ritual and Magic*, p. 133.

20 *The Revelation of St John the Divine*, 2:17.

21 Wilfred Bouser, 'Magical Practices against Elves', *Folklore* Part 4:37, 1936, pp. 353–9.

22 J. Hope, *In Pendle's Shadow*, 1994, p. 7.

23 Thomas Potts, *Discoverie*, p. 150.

24 Undated document, Local History File, Chatburn Library.

25 For those too young to remember, in pre-decimal coinage 'd' stood for penny, derived from the Roman coin the *denarius*.

26 J. B. Taylor, 'The Witchposts of Rossendale', p. 18.

27 Personal Communication: Ralph Merrifield to Jennie Cobban, 4th April 1989.

28 Letter from M. N. Petch, Manchester Museum to Ralph Merrifield, 19th May 1989. Although it is recorded there, the Manchester Museum does not appear to hold photographs of the head as I had hoped. (Personal communication via email: Bryan Sitch, Head of Human Cultures, Manchester Museum, 17th September 2010.) Unfortunately this means that the only photograph of this interesting feature is one I did not send to Dr Merrifield due to its rather inferior quality.

29 John Billingsley, *Stony Gaze*, 1998.

30 There may be some link between stone heads and the various sacred, or occasionally 'screaming' skulls which are to be found in some Lancashire properties, e.g. that at Browsholme Hall. These skulls seem to be quite happy in the house as long as they are left alone, but heaven forbid that you try to remove or disturb one because then all hell will break loose. This may reflect the dual nature of both the stone head and the skull (and possibly also concealed shoes). Once they have been recruited as protective devices, the objects do not seem to like interference.

31 Personal communication: Ralph Merrifield to Jennie Cobban, 25th August 1990.

32 John Billingsley, *Stony Gaze*, pp. 89–90.

33 A. Smith, 'Celtic Heads', *Where Rivers Meet*, Vol. 2: No. 2, Whalley and District Historical and Archaeological Society, Winter 1989, p. 20.

34 M. Yates, 'More Blood on the Stairs; A new Version of Lamkin', 11th November 2004, http://www.mustrad.org.uk/articles/lamkin.htm.

35 *Dorset Evening Echo*, 22nd December 1987 and http://www.apotropaios.co.uk/dorset_survey.htm.

36 A. Smith, 'Celtic Heads', p. 11.

37 Thomas Potts, *Discoverie*, p. 18.

38 There is another very attractive little stonepit near the Boggart's Well on Jinny Lane that is actually closer to Newchurch than Faugh's quarry, and which may be identified as an alternative site for Demdike's first meeting with Tibb. A friendly farmer working nearby also informed me that this little quarry was the older of the two.

39 It is said that the 'Eye of God' is actually a filled-in window through which the

sexton used to watch out for approaching funeral processions. When he spotted them arriving he would alert the bell ringer below who would begin to toll the passing bell. (See Clifford H. Byrne, *Newchurch in Pendle: Folklore, Fact and Fiction*, p. 18.)

40 Personal Communication: Ralph Merrifield to Jennie Cobban, 13th May, 1990.

41 Ralph Merrifield, *The Archaeology of Ritual and Magic*, pp. 117–19, 124–5. It is also interesting to note that Stiperden Moor, to the north of the Long Causeway above Cliviger, is known as 'place of the skulls'. According to Thomas Dunham Whitaker in *History of the Original Parish of Whalley and Honor of Clitheroe* , Vol. 2, p. 212, 'One practical superstition, peculiar so far as I know to this place [Cliviger], deserves to be remembered. The hydrocephalus is a disease incident to adolescent animals, and is supposed by the shepherds and herdsmen to be contagious: but, in order to prevent the progress of the disease, whenever a young beast had died of this complaint, it was usual, and it has, I believe, been practised by farmers still alive, to cut off the head and convey it for interment into the nearest part of the adjoining county. Stiperden, a desert place upon the borders of Yorkshire, was the place of skulls.' There is a possibility, of course, that this is a rationalisation of an older custom with a more ritualistic and sacrificial origin. See also J. Billingsley, 'Medical Care, Magical Cure', *Northern Earth* 86, 2001, pp. 11–16, http://www. northernearth.co.uk/medcare.htm

42 If Doctor Webster did indeed live at Great Mitton Hall, it could only have been for a few months. He was presented to the living in Mitton in 1648, and was a registered householder in Clitheroe from late 1649 until his death in 1682. In Clitheroe, Webster lived in Study House on Church Street near St Mary Magdalene's church where he was eventually buried. The house has been re-fronted and added to, but parts of the original fabric are thought to survive. Also surviving within the church is Webster's curious brass memorial through which he hints to posterity that he was confident he had achieved 'grace' (i.e. a oneness with God) through his Christian alchemical experiments.

Endnotes Chapter 4

1   Thomas Shadwell, *The Lancashire Witches*, Act III, 1691.

2   Dr John Webster, *The Displaying of Supposed Witchcraft*, chap. 2, Clitheroe Community History Collection, 1676, p. 29.

3   Thomas Potts, *Discoverie*, pp. 153–4.

4   Ibid. p. 158.

5   Lancashire Record Office, QSB/1/139 (81).

6   Lancashire Record Office, QSB/1/139 (81).

7   Owen Davies, 'Charmers and Charming in England and Wales from the

Eighteenth to the Twentieth Century', *Folklore* 1–09, 1988, p. 44.

8   Quoted in Montague Summers, *Witchcraft and Black Magic*, 1945, p. 17.

9   For a full discussion of this charm see Jonathan Lumby, *The Lancashire Witch Craze*, 1995, pp. 93–4.

10   Thomas Potts, *Discoverie*, pp. 42–3.

11   Lancashire Record Office, QSB 1/202/89.

12   For the full story see Owen Davies, *Cunning-Folk*, 2003, pp. 43–5.

13   James Standing, 'Old Langsettle (or GOLD LEGS) and the claimants that he duped', *Recollections from a Lancashire Vale*, 1885.

14   Owen Davies, *Cunning-folk: Popular Magic in English History*, p. 136.

15   Dr Webster rails against the northern propensity to require 'charms with everything'. (See Dr John Webster, *Displaying of Supposed Witchcraft*, chap. XVI, pp. 323–4.)

16   W. Self Weeks, 'A Lancashire Charm' (reprinted from *Transactions of the Lancashire and Cheshire Antiquarian Society*, Vol. XXVII, 1910). See also, Ralph Merrifield, *The Archaeology of Ritual and Magic*, pp. 148–50.

17   'A Charm or Exorcism Against Witchcraft & Evil Spirits', *The Reliquary Quarterly*, Vol. VI (New Series), January 1892, pp. 534–5.

18   G. Dodds, 'The Translation of an Ancient Formula of Magical Exorcism, written in cipher', *The Reliquary Quarterly*, January, 1870.

19   James I, *Demonologie*, pp. 59, 67.

20   Documents and illustrations in Pendle Witch Exhibition File 1972, Towneley Hall Museum.

21   Tattersall Wilkinson, 'Folklore', *Transactions of the Burnley Literary and Scientific Society*, Vol. 13, 1896, pp. 51–60.

22   Ibid.

23   Reginald Scot, *The Discoverie of Witchcraft*, book XII: chap. 14, 1584 (reprinted by Dover Publications, 1972, p. 140).

24   C. Moorhouse, *Sabden, the Forgotten Valley*, 1978, p. 93.

25   Lancashire Record Office, DDX/471/1.

26   James L. Maxim 'Discovery of two charms against Evil Spirits at Cross Lees, Syke, Rochdale and Meadow Head, Norden'. (Lecture notes, read February 1921, Local Studies Library, Touchstones, Rochdale).

27   Handwritten document, 'A charm against evil spirits found at Meadow Head, near Wolstenholme Hall, Norden', Local Studies Library, Touchstones, Rochdale.

28   W. G. Black, *Folk Medicine: a Chapter in the History of Culture*, Folklore Society, 1883, p. 170.

29   'Cal. of State Papers (Dom), 1595–7', p406. (Quoted in C. L'Estrange Ewan, *Witchcraft and Demonology*, 1933, p. 408.)

30   Manchester Sessions before Sir Cecil Trafford and others on 23rd January 1623 in C. L'Estrange Ewan, *Witchcraft and Demonology*, p. 408.

31 Lancashire Record Office, QSB 1/255/38.

32 General Quarter Sessions of the Peace at Manchester, 14ᵗʰ October 1680 (P.L 26/22) Quoted in C. L'Estrange Ewan, *Witchcraft and Demonology*, p. 413.

33 W. Robertson, *Old and New Rochdale*, 1881, ttp://www.link4life.org/index. cfm?fuseaction=c.showPage&pageID=594.

34 Harland and Wilkinson, *Lancashire Witchcraft, Charms and Spells*, pp. 1–2.

35 Clifford H. Byrne, *Newchurch in Pendle: Folklore, Fact and Fiction*, p. 13.

36 Letter to Editor from Frank Kirkby, Levenshulme, Manchester. (Published in *The Dalesman*, Issue 26, 1964, p. 333.)

37 E. Sibley, *A New & Complete Illustration of the Occult Sciences*, book 4, 1784, http:// www.esotericarchives.com/solomon/sibly4.htm.

38 Joseph Blagrave of Reading in his *Astrological Practice of Physick*, 1671, pp. 154–5 gives an explanation of how it all works: '*Another way is to stop the urine of the Patient, close up in a bottle, and put into it three nails, pins or needles, with a little white salt, keeping the urine always warm: if you let it remain long in the bottle, it will endanger the witch's life: for I have found by experience that they will be grievously tormented making their water with great difficulty, if any at all, and the more if the Moon be in Scorpio in Square or Opposition to his Significator, when its done.*' He then explains the reasoning behind the operation: '*The reason ... is because there is part of the vital spirit of the Witch in it, for such is the subtlety of the Devil, that he will not suffer the Witch to infuse any poisonous matter into the body of man or beast, without some of the Witches blood mingled with it ...* ' (Quoted in Ralph Merrifield, *The Archaeology of Ritual and Magic*, pp. 169–70.)

39 J. Glanvill, *Sadducismus Triumphatus*, 1681, (Quoted in Ralph Merrifield, *The Archaeology of Ritual and Magic*, pp. 171–2.)

40 The Confession of Margaret Johnson, http:/www.pendlewitches.co.uk/content. php?page=Margaret.

41 Richard Catlow, *The Pendle Witches*, p. 35.

42 Letter in witchcraft exhibition file, 1972, Towneley Hall Museum, and personal communication with Heather Millard, Museums Officer, Social History, Cliffe Castle Museum, Keighley.

Endnotes Chapter 5

1 Thomas Heywood, and Richard Brome, 'The Witches of Lancashire', Act IV: Scene 1 (Edmund Robinson's speech), 1634, in *Globe Quartos*, Nick Hern Books Ltd., 2002.

2 Presumably Christopher Holgate, Demdike's son.

3 Edmund's story seems to have influenced and inspired a young female witchfinder from Northumbria called Anne Armstrong, who, in 1673 claimed to have been

transformed into a beast of burden and ridden to a witches' feast. She also said the witches at the feast obtained food by pulling on ropes. (See C. L'Estrange Ewan, *Witchcraft and Demonology*, pp. 358–61.)

4　*A History of the Parish of Fence*, Fence Parochial Church Council, 1934, p. 13. The spot was still known as Boggart Hole in 1845 according to Thomas Potts, *Discoverie*, Chetham Society, 1845, Introduction p. Lxiii.

5　This really does not say much for the perspicacity of the two J Ps, Richard Shuttleworth and John Starkie.

6　*Calendar of State Papers Domestic*, 1634–5, p. 26. (Quoted in M. Tonge, 'The Lancashire Witches: 1612 and 1634', *Transactions of the Historic Society of Lancashire & Cheshire*, LXXXIII, 1931, p. 161.)

7　British Museum, Add MS. 36674, f. 197. (Quoted in C. L'Estrange Ewan, *Witchcraft and Demonology*, pp. 246–7.)

8　Confession of Margaret Johnson in Thomas Potts, *Discoverie*, pp. lxxii-lxxv. Chetham Society, 1845.

9　Dr John Webster, chap. V, p. 82 .

10　The presiding judges would have been George Vernon and Francis Crawley. (See J. S. Cockburn, *A History of the English Assizes 1558–1714*, 1972, p. 271.)

11　M. Tonge, 'The Lancashire Witches: 1612 and 1634', p. 161.

12　Alison Findlay, 'Sexual and Spiritual Politics in the events of 1633–4 and the Late Lancashire Witches', *The Lancashire Witches: Histories and Stories*, 2002, pp. 148–9.

13　At a witch trial in Malmesbury, John Aubrey commented that, 'The crowd of spectators made such a noise that the Judge could not heare the Prisoner, nor the Prisoner the Judge; but the words were handed from one to the other by Mr R Chandler, and sometimes not truly reported'. (Quoted in G. Durston, *A History of English Witchcraft and its Legal Perspectives 1542–1736*, 2000, p. 390.)

14　Lancashire Record Office, DDKE/acc.7840 HMC/380, 1679–80. ' … that the Judges are dissatisfied to keep the Assizes at Lancaster, in respect of the ruines of the castle at Lancaster, conceiving some danger to sitt there untill the same be repaired … '

15　http://www.londononline.co.uk/history/thames/10/ and www.thegreenwich-phantom.co.uk/ … /the-witch-the-bucket-and-the-very-naughty-boy (A comment posted on this website made the suggestion that one of the Lancashire witches might have been responsible for the Cutty Sark catching fire!)

16　Sir William Brereton, *Travels in Holland, the United Provinces, England, Scotland & Ireland 1634–5*, No. 1, Chetham Society, pp. 33–4.

17　*Old and New London: Volume 2*, 'The Fleet Prison', 1878, pp. 404–16, http://www.british-history.ac.uk/report.aspx?compid=45111, accessed 31st December 2010.

18　Dr John Webster, chap. XVII, p. 346.

19　*Calendar State Papers Domestic*, 1634–5, p. 129.

20 *Gentleman's Magazine*, 1832, pp. 407–8 and Cathy Gere, 'William Harvey's Weak Experiment: the archaeology of an anecdote', *History Workshop Journal*, Vol.51, 2001, pp. 19–36.

21 C. L'Estrange Ewan, *Witchcraft and Demonology*, p. 251.

22 *A History of the County of Lancaster: Volume 6*, 'Townships: Goldshaw Booth', 1911, footnote 17, accessed 16th February 2010.

23 Lancashire Record Office, DDF 2437/31.

24 John A. Clayton, *The Lancashire Witch Conspiracy*, 2007, p. 220.

25 Lancashire Record Office, QSP 165/12 (Lancashire Quarter Sessions records.)

26 *A Narration of the Life of Mr Henry Burton*, 1643, (quoted in *Bygone Lancashire*, 1892, pp. 60–61).

27 *The Leeds Mercury*, Answers and Comments: 'The Lancashire Witches' (Query No. 1, 30th March), Saturday 31st December 1887.

28 I have been unable to independently confirm these details.

29 M. Swisher, 'Beyond the Hoar Stone', *Neophilologus* 86, 2002, p. 133.

30 Ibid. p. 133.

31 Thomas Potts, *Discoverie*, Introduction, pp. lxii-lxiii, Chetham Society, 1845.

32 *A History of the Parish of Fence*, p. 13.

33 Alison Findlay, 'Sexual and Spiritual Politics', *The Lancashire Witches: Histories and Stories*, 2002, p. 151.

Endnotes Chapter 6

1   Old song, possibly by J. B. Geoghegan, (quoted in John Harland, *Ballads and Songs of Lancashire, Ancient and Modern*, 1875, pp. 205–6.)

2   Thomas Heywood and Richard Brome, 'The Witches of Lancashire', in *Globe Quartos*, Nick Hern Books, 2002.

3   Berry, 'The Globe Bewitched', in *Medieval and Renaissance Drama in England 1*, 1984, p. 214.

4   Ibid. pp. 212–13.

5   Thomas Heywood, and Richard Brome, 'The Witches of Lancashire', in *Globe Quartos*, p. 94.

6   W. Van Lennep, 'The Earliest Known English Playbill', *Harvard Library Bulletin*, Part 3, 1947, p. 385.

7   'News From Hyde Park', (Stanza 11), *English Dance and Song*, Vol. 64: Part 1.

8   'The Lancashire Witches', *The Palatine Garland*. (A selection of Ballads and Fragments supplementary to The Palatine Anthology, 1850, pp. 64–7.)

9   W. Van Lennep, 'The Earliest Known English Playbill', pp. 382–5.

10 For a discussion of the type of music considered appropriate for stage witches, see

Amanda Eubanks Winkler, *O Let us Howle Some Heavy Note: Music for Witches, the Melancholic and the Mad on the Seventeenth Century Stage*, 2007, pp. 18–63.

11 Ibid. pp. 22–3.

12 Philip H. Highfill, *A Biographical Dictionary of Actors*, Vol. 4, 1973.

13 *Weekly Packet*, Issue 465, London, Saturday, 27th May 1721.

14 *Spectator*, Issue CXLI, 11th August 1711.

15 *Public Advertiser*, Issue 7068, Tuesday, 21st June 1757.

16 The woodcuts used seem to vary with different editions of the pamphlet.

17 The Rivals/Lancashire Witches playbill, Manchester Central Library, Theatre Collection, Class: Th 792.094273 Ma105.

18 *Public Advertiser*, Issue 15468, Wednesday 24th December 1783.

19 'The songs in the new pantomime called The Lancashire Witches: or the distresses of Harlequin 1783', electronic resource, National Library of Australia.

20 W. Drayton, *Poly-Olbion*, Song 23, 1622.

21 *World*, Issue 703, Tuesday 31st March 1789.

22 Thomas Potts, *Discoverie*, Chetham Society, 1845, p. Lii.

23 For a full discussion of Harrison Ainsworth and his career, see Jeffrey Richards, 'The Lancashire Novelist and the Lancashire witches' in *The Lancashire Witches: Histories and Stories*, 2002.

24 *The Era*, Issue 588, London, Sunday, 30th December 1849.

25 We have of course met Tim Bobbin, aka John Collier, before, when he blew up the Prickshaw Witch with gunpowder!

26 *Liverpool Mercury*, Issue 2358, Tuesday, 30th December 1851.

27 *Liverpool Mercury*, Thursday 29th December 1864.

28 R. J. Broadbent, *Annals of the Liverpool Stage*, 1908, p. 301.

29 An old Lancashire term for a 'Liverpool man'.

30 *Liverpool Mercury*, Issue 5897, Saturday 22nd December 1866.

31 *The Times*, Wednesday 4th August 1858. Bram Stoker, the creator of Dracula, was the Business Manager of this theatre from 1878–98.

32 *The Era*, Issue 1954, London, Sunday 5th March 1876.

33 *The Era*, Issue 1954, London, Sunday 5th March 1876.

34 *Manchester Times*, Saturday 21st January 1853.

35 Ibid. 29th January 1870.

36 *Reynold's Newspaper*, Issue 2007, London, Sunday 27th January 1889.

37 *Liverpool Mercury*, Issue 6618, Monday 12th April 1869.

38 http://www.britishmuseum.org/research/search_the_collection_database/search_object_image.aspx, accessed on 27th January 2011. The engraving held by the British Museum, in which the girl wears a jewelled headband, appears to differ from the original painting where the girl is wearing a hat.

39 *Gentleman's Magazine* ii, 116, 1867.

40 http://www.spartacus.schoolnet.co.uk/RAlancashire.htm.

41 Search for 'Lancashire Witch Locomotive' on *canvasstorehouse.com*

42 http://en.wikipedia.org/wiki/File:86213_'Lancashire_Witch'_at_Crewe_Works.

43 *Daily Gazetteer*, Saturday 21st February 1741.

44 *Public Ledger* or *The Daily Register of Commerce & Intelligence*, Friday 26th June 1761.

45 http://members.aceweb.com/ronsmith/liverpool/ships_l.htm, and P. Aughton, *Liverpool, A People's History*.

46 http://www.liverpoolmuseums.org.uk/ism/slavery/middle_passage/john_newton. aspx.

47 http://www.rootsweb.ancestry.com/~nzlscant/LANwitchdiaryshepherd.htm.

48 http://www.melbourne-australia-maps.com/SS-Coogee.html.

Endnotes Chapter 7

1 Doreen Valiente, *The Witches' Creed*, http://www.sacred-texts.com/bos/bos083. htm.

2 Two world wars did, of course, make it increasingly difficult to hold this historical world view.

3 http://collections.lancsmuseums.gov.uk/narratives/narrative.php?irn=193.

4 http://collections.lancsmuseums.gov.uk/narratives/narrative.php?irn=221

5 *Clitheroe Advertiser and Times*, Friday 3rd May 1935.

6 It is very noticeable that church groups in the early twentieth century seemed to have no problem whatsoever with their young people dressing up as witches.

7 Sue Holden, *Clitheroe Ablaze with Glory*, 1999, p. 41.

8 Margaret Murray, *The Witch Cult in Western Europe*, 1921 and *The God of the Witches*, 1933. Most of Murray's witchcraft theories have now been thoroughly discredited by modern historians.

9 For an excellent study of Gardner, see Philip Heselton's *Gerald Gardner and the Cauldron of Inspiration*, 2003.

10 Lois Bourne, *Witch Amongst Us*, 1979, *Conversations with a Witch*, 1989, *Dancing with Witches*, 1998, *Spells to Change your Life*, 2003.

11 Notably Edgar Peel and Pat Southern in the 1960s.

12 Personal communications with the author.

13 Terry Pratchett's fabulous Lancre Witches call it 'headology'.

14 June Johns, *King of the Witches: The World of Alex Sanders*, 1969, pp. 95–7.

15 Published as *The Elegant Witch* in the United States.

16 Letter from Robert Neill to Mr Blundell, Curator, Towneley Hall, 7th May 1972.

17 Thanks to Laurence Inwood, BBC Manchester, for providing a DVD of the production.

18 Unfortunately the education system has so far failed to recover from the problems

caused at this time by fundamentalist Christian groups. Their insistence on the reality of a fictitious satanic conspiracy (and invention of evidence to support such delusions) has left us with a legacy of reluctance to allow children access to information about witchcraft in an historical context. This represents, in my opinion, totally unacceptable censorship and as such should be resisted vigorously whenever certain minorities attempt to dictate what should and should not be taught in schools. (See P. Jenkins, 'The Devil Rides In: Charismatic Christians and the Depiction of a Satanic Menace in contemporary Britain', *Religiologiques* 11, Spring 1995, pp. 169–92.

19 Personal communication: Alice Nutter via Facebook, 30th January 2011.

20 Jean Walton, *Pendle Forest Folk*, 1977, pp. 47.

21 Clifford H. Byrne, *Newchurch in Pendle: Folklore, Fact and Fiction*, 1982, p. 28.

22 Visitors may also visit the alleged grave of Jennet Preston at St Mary the Virgin Church at Gisburn.

23 Letter from Cecil Williamson to Mr Blundel, Curator, Towneley Hall, 10th November 1971 and conversations with the author 1990–91.

24 E. Peel and P. Southern, *The Trials of the Lancashire Witches*, pp. 148–9

25 http://www.salemwitchmuseum.com/tour.

26 Thomas Shadwell, *The Lancashire Witches*, Act II, Song of Demdike and her witches, 1691.

Bibliography

'A Charm or Exorcism against Witchcraft & Evil Spirits', *The Reliquary Quarterly*,
  Vol. VI (New Series), January 1892

A History of Lancaster Castle, 1882

*A History of Lancaster Castle, with an Account of its Remarkable prisoners and of many
  Extraordinary Executions*, 1882

Ainsworth, W. H., *The Lancashire Witches: A Romance of Pendle Forest*, 1884

Aughton, P., *Liverpool, A People's History*, 2003

Axon, E., *Bygone Lancashire*, 1892

Bernard, R., *A Guide to the Grand-Jury Men*, 1627

Berry, H., 'The Globe Bewitched', *Medieval and Renaissance Drama in England*, 1 (1984)

Billingsley, J., 'Medical Care, Magical Cure', *Northern Earth* 86, 2001

Billingsley, J., *Stony Gaze: Investigating Celtic & other Stone Heads*, 1998

Black, W. G., 'Folk Medicine: a Chapter in the History of Culture', *Folklore*, 1883

Borrow, G. H., *Romano Lavo Lil (Romany Dictionary)*, 1874

Bouser, W., 'Magical Practices against Elves', *Folklore* Part 4:37, 1936

Broadbent, R. J., *Annals of the Liverpool Stage*, 1908

Byrne, C. H., *Newchurch in Pendle: Folklore, Fact and Fiction*, 1982

Byrne, C. H., *The Cross and the Cauldron: A Witches' book of lore spells and charms*, 1986

Catlow, R., *The Pendle Witches*, 1976

Cavendish, R., *The Black Arts*, 1977

Clayton, J. A. *The Lancashire Witch Conspiracy*, 2007

Cobban, J. L., *Geoffrey de Mandeville and London's Camelot: Ghosts, Mysteries and the
  Occult in Barnet*, 1997

Cockburn, J. S. and Green, T., *Twelve Good Men and True: The Criminal Trial Jury in
  England 1200–1800*, 1988

Cockburn, J. S., *A History of the English Assizes*, 1972

Cohn, N., *Europe's Inner Demons*, 1975

Coleridge, S.T., *The Rime of the Ancient Mariner*, 1798

Court Rolls of the Honour of Clitheroe in the County of Lancaster, 1912

Crossley, J., *Potts' Discovery of Witches in the County of Lancaster*, Remains Historical
  and Literary connected with the Palatine counties of Lancaster and Chester, The
  Chetham Society, 1845

Davies, O., 'Charmers and Charming in England and Wales from the Eighteenth to the
  Twentieth Century', *Folklore* 1–09, 1988

Davies, O., *Cunning-Folk: Popular Magic in English History*, 2003

Dendy Marshall, C. F., *A History of Railway Locomotives down to the end of the year 1831*, 1953

Dodds, G., 'The Translation of an Ancient Formula of Magical Exorcism, written in Cipher', *The Reliquary Quarterly*, January 1870

Drayton, W., *Poly-Olbion*, 1622

Durston, G., *Witchcraft and Witch Trials: A History of English Witchcraft and its Legal Perspectives*, 2009

Ewan, C. L'Estrange, *Witchcraft and Demonology*, 1933

Fairfax, E., *Demonologia: A Discourse on Witchcraft as it was acted in the family of Mr Edward Fairfax*, 1622, (2007 edition, publisher unknown)

Farone, C., 'What's New in Ancient Roman Magic: Recent Archaeological Discoveries', *Amphora*, Vol. 5: Issue 2

Fleury, C., *Time-Honoured Lancaster: Historic Notes on the Ancient Borough of Lancaster*, 1891

Harland J. and Wilkinson, T. T., *Lancashire Legends, Traditions, Pageants, Sports etc.*, 1873

Harland, J. and Wilkinson, T. T., *Lancashire Witchcraft, Charms and Spells*, (originally published as *Lancashire Folklore*, 1882)

Harland, J., *Ballads and Songs of Lancashire, Ancient and Modern*, 1875

Henderson, W., *Notes on the Folklore of the Northern Counties of England and the Borders*, 1879

Herrick, R., *Hesperides*, 1648

Heselton, P., *Gerald Gardner and the Cauldron of Inspiration*, 2003

Heywood, T., and Brome, R., *The Witches of Lancashire 1634* in the Globe Quartos, 2002

Hickey, S., 'Fatal Feeds?: Livestock Losses and Witchcraft Accusations in Tudor and Stuart England', *Folklore* Vol. 101: II, 1990

Highfill, P. H., *A Biographical Dictionary of Actors*, Vol. 4, 1973

Hill, F., *A Delusion of Satan: The Full Story of the Salem Witch Trials*, 1995

Holden, S., *Clitheroe Ablaze with Glory*, 1999

Hope, J., *In Pendle's Shadow*, 1994

James I of England, *Daemonologie*, 1597 (The Book Tree edition, 2002, published as *Demonology*)

James, R., *Iter Lanastriense*, 1636

Jenkins, P., 'The Devil Rides in: Charismatic Christians and the Depiction of a Satanic Menace in Contemporary Britain', *Religiologiques* 11, Spring 1995

Johns, J., *King of the Witches: The World of Alex Sanders*, 1969

Kennerley, E., *Thomas Covell of Lancaster, Esquire*, Local Studies No. 11, Lancaster City Museum, n.d.

Kirk, R., *The Secret Commonwealth of Elves, Fauns and Fairies, 1691*, New York Review Books, 2007

Lang, J. B., 'Charming of Cattle', *Proceedings of the Dorset Natural History & Archaeology Society 91*, 1969

Laycock, J. A., *Pendle Forest Witches: A Lecture by Dr Laycock of Sabden*, n.d.

Logan, J., *The Prediction Book of Amulets and Talismans*, 1986

Lumby, J., *The Lancashire Witch Craze*, 1995

Maxim, J. L., *Discovery of Two Charms against Evil Spirits at Cross Lees, Syke, Rochdale and Meadow Head, Norden*, Lecture Notes 1921 and handwritten manuscript *A Charm against Evil Spirits found at Meadow Head, near Wolstenholme Hall, Norden*, (Local Studies Library, Rochdale)

McKay, J., *Pendle Hill in History and Literature*, 1888

Merrifield, R., *The Archaeology of Ritual and Magic*, 1987

Moorhouse, C., *Sabden, The Forgotten Valley*, 1978

Murray, M., *The God of the Witches*, 1933

Murray, M., *The Witch Cult in Western Europe*, 1921

Nattrass, M., 'Witch posts and Early Dwellings in Cleveland', *Yorkshire Archaeological Journal*, 1956 and 'Witch posts', *Gwerin*, Vol. 3, 1962

Neill, R., *Mist over Pendle*, 1951

'Newes from Scotland' (pamphlet), 1591, (The Book Tree edition, 2002)

'News from Hyde Park', Stanza 11, English Dance and Song, Vol. 64:Part 1:No. 1, 1885

Opie, I. and Tatem, M. (Eds), *A Dictionary of Superstitions*, 1989

Peel, E. and Southern, P., *The Trials of the Lancashire Witches*, 1969

'Rawtenstall House with a Witch post', *Rossendale Free Press*, 1967

Register Transcripts, Lancashire Parish Register Society, Vol. 32: Baptism, Marriage, Burial, 1599–1690

Remy, N., *Demonolatry: An Account of the Historical Practice of Witchcraft, 1595*, Dover Publications, 2008

Richards, J., 'The Lancashire Novelist and the Lancashire Witches', *The Lancashire Witches: Histories and Stories* (Ed. Poole, R.), 2002

Robertson, W., *Old and New Rochdale*, 1881

Scot, R., *The Discoverie of Witchcraft, 1584*, Dover Publications, 1972

Self Weeks, W., 'A Lancashire Charm', *Transactions of the Lancashire and Cheshire Antiquarian Society*, Vol. XXVII, 1910

Self Weeks, W., *Clitheroe in the Seventeenth Century*, n.d.

Shadwell, T., 'The Lancashire Witches, and Tegue o Divelly the Irish Priest. A Comedy. Part the first (in five acts and in prose). The Amorous Bigot, with the second part of Tegue o Divelly, a comedy', 1691, (Historical Collection from the British Library, digitalised image), www.bl.uk, n.d

Shakespeare, W., *Macbeth*, 1603–7

Sibley, E., *A New and Complete Illustration of the Occult Sciences*, book 4, 1784, http://www.esotericarchives.com/solomon/sibly4.htm.

Simpson, J. and Roud, S., *Oxford Dictionary of English Folklore*, 2003

Smith, A., 'Celtic Heads', *Where Rivers Meet*, Vol. 2: No. 2, Whalley and District Historical and Archaeological Society, Winter 1989

Songs etc. in the New Pantomime called The Lancashire Witches: or the distresses of Harlequin, 1783, National Library of Australia

Spicer, H., *The Witch Wife, a Tale of Malkin Tower*, 1849

Standing, J., 'Old Langsettle (or GOLD LEGS) and the claimants that he duped', *Recollections from a Lancashire Vale*, 1885

Summers, M., *Witchcraft and Black Magic*, 1945

Swain, J., 'Witchcraft, Economy and Society', *The Lancashire Witches: Histories and Stories* (Ed. Poole, R.), 2002

Taylor, J. B., 'The Witch posts of Rossendale', *Valley Magazine*, June 1988

The Dalesman, Issue 26, 1964, p. 333

'The Famous History of the Lancashire Witches: Containing their manner of becoming such' (pamphlet), circa 1780.

'The Folk-Lore of Drayton', Part 4: Local Traditions, Proverbs (Continued), *FolkLore*, Vol. 3

The House and Farm Accounts of the Shuttleworths of Gawthorpe Hall, Chetham Society, 1856

'The Lancashire Witches', *The Palatine Garland* (A selection of Ballads and Fragments supplementary to The Palatine Anthology), 1850

The Lancaster Martyrs, Incorporated Catholic Truth Society, n.d.

The Mad Pranks and Merrie Jests of Robin Goodfellow, (reprinted for the Percy Society from the edition of 1628), 1841.

The Pictorial History of the County of Lancaster, 1844

'The Wood of Thor was a Guard Against Witches', *Burnley Evening Star*, 1972

'The Pendle Witches: A Trial in Seventeenth Century Lancashire', Towneley Hall exhibition files, 1972

Valiente, D., *The Witches' Creed*, http://www.sacred-texts.com

Van Lennep, W., 'The Earliest Known English Playbill', *Harvard Library Bulletin*, Part 3, 1947

Walton, J., *Pendle Forest Folk*, 1977

Webster, J., *The Displaying of Supposed Witchcraft*, 1676

Webster, N., *Halls and Manor Houses of North East Lancashire*, 2003

Whitaker, T. D., *History of the Original Parish of Whalley and Honour of Clitheroe*, Vol. 2, 1872

Whittaker, G., *Rough Lee Hall – Fact and Fiction*, 1980

Wilby, E., *Cunning Folk and Familiar Spirits: Shamanistic Visionary Traditions in Early Modern British Witchcraft and Magic*, 2005

Wilkinson, T., 'Folklore', *Transactions of the Burnley Literary and Scientific Society*, Vol. 13, 1896

Winkler, A. E., *O Let us Howle Some Heavy Note: Music for Witches, the Melancholic and the Mad on the Seventeenth Century Stage*, 2007

Yates, M., *More Blood on the Stairs: A new version of Lamkin*, 2004

Index

Page numbers in italics refer to illustrations.

AC Locomotive group 130

Acorah, Derek 143

Ainsworth, Harrison 32, 125, *125*

all-seeing eye of God, St Mary's church 67, *69*

Altham 4, 17

Altham, Sir James 13, 14

Anna Perenna (Roman goddess) 28

Archangel Michael 79

Aspinall Arms, Mitton 53

Aspull 77

Assheton, Edmund 75, 76

Baggilie, Henry (wise-man/charmer) 75–6

Baker, Ann 111

Ball (familiar spirit of Elizabeth Device) 29, 40

ballads about Lancashire witches 118, 127

Bank Hall, Barrowford 66

Bannister, Nicholas 3–4, 17

Barnoldswick 136

Barrett, John 118

Bartholomew Fair 118

Beech Grove, Chatburn 68

   strange incidents 58–61

Belphegor 87, 88

Berry, Mr 37

Billingsley, John 62, 63

Birkenhead 139

Bobbin, Tim (John Collier) 77, 126

body searches for witch marks 101–2

boggart 96, 144

Boggart Hole 96

Bolton-by-Bowland 54

Bothwell, Earl Francis 28

Bourne, Lois *137*, 138

Bowland, Trough of 8, *9*, 64

Bradley, William 128, 129

Brand, Henig 90

Brereton, Sir Thomas 104

Bridgeman, John

   ordered by king to examine witches 102–3

   sends witch report to king 104

   1635 examines more witches 112

Brierley, Roger 103

Brigantia 49

British Museum 78

Bromley, Sir Edward *12*, 13, 14, 17

   bus 146

Brungerley 36–7

Brungerley Farm 37–8

bucranium 70–1, *71*

Bulcock, John and Jane 5, 16

   impenitent at gallows 19

Bulhof 42–3

Bull Hole Farm 42, 43–4, *44*, *45*, 46–7, 66, 83

Burnley 33, 100, 103, 130, 144

   astrological charm against witchcraft 81

Burton, Henry 12, 112

Butterworth 86

Calder, River *139*, 140

Castleton 85, 86

Catlow, Richard 2

cattle, bewitching of 33–4, 43–5, 77, 84, 109

ceremony of the gallows 16, 18

Chadderton 75

Chadwick, Anne *see* Chattox (Mother)

Charles I, King
   fascinated by Lancashire witches 102
   meets the Lancashire witches 108

charms (written) against witchcraft 75–6,
   76–7, 78–88, *80*, 88
   Burnley 81, 86–7
   Daubers Farm, Foulridge, near Colne 81
   farmer's effects, found in *88*, 88–9
   Healey, Mrs (Burnley) 81
   Healey, Rochdale 81
   Paracelsian charm 82–5, *83*
   purchaser, not to be read by 85
   Simonstone 87–8
   tombstone, found under 81
   West Bradford 78–80, *80*

Chatburn 58–62, 68

Chattox, Elizabeth 43

Chattox (Mother) 2, 3, 4, 5, 16, 18, 29, 57
   bewitches John Nutter's and John Moore's
      cows to death 43
   changes her story in prison 40–1
   charm to amend drink 76–7
   churns milk at Bull Hole 43
   hides clay picture from Alizon 28–9
   removes teeth from Newchurch graveyard
      30
   shares teeth with Demdike 30
   wise-woman, in role of 76–7

Chetham Society 124, 125

Chohawniskey tem (witches' country) 25

christening the spirit 7

Chumbawamba 144

circle-dancing 38–9

clay pictures (voodoo dolls) 27, *27*, 28–32

Clegg, George 77

Cliffe Castle Museum, Keighley 33

Clitheroe 17, 25, 42, 58, 78, 96, 113, *130*, *135*,
   136

Clitheroe Castle Museum 53

Clitheroe pageants (1935 and 1948) *135*, 136

Cold Light Singing 144

Collier, John (Tim Bobbin of Rochdale) 77,
   126

Colne Field 3

Colne murderer commits suicide 19

comic characters, witches as 105, 117–18, 119,
   121, 126
   see also Lancashire witches: comic opera

concealed shoes 53–5, *54*
   Aspinall Arms, Mitton 53, *54*
   associated objects 53, 55
   children's clogs, Fooden Cottage 54
   Clitheroe Castle Museum 53
   fertility associations 53
   human sacrifice, alternative to 54
   removal results in haunting 55
   Schorn, John, associated with 54
   Talbot Head Hotel, Strawclough 53
   Yealand Conyers 53, *54*, 55

Coogee, SS (originally the *Lancashire Witch*)
   132

Cornelius Agrippa 78

Court of Assize 13–17, *14*
   commences Monday, 17th August 13
   ends on Wednesday, 19th August 16
   no individual trials 14
   courthouse in Lancaster Castle, poor repair
      of 103

Covell, Thomas 5, 6, 11–13, 40, 41, 100

Cox, Susannah 119

Cromwell, Oliver 118

Cronkshaw, Jennet 110, 112

Cross Keys, Lancaster 18

Cross Lees, Syke 84

Crow Trees Cottage, Worston 32

Crowley, Aleister 136

Cunningham, John see Fian, Doctor

Cutty Sark 104

Daemonologie (King James I) 15, 16, 30, 39, 81

dancing the Tyburn jig 21

Dandy (familiar spirit of James Device) 41

Danoine Sith 35

Delaney, Joseph 142

Demdike (Mother) 1–2, 4, 5, 16, 23, 27, 30,
    40, 43–4, 67, 125–6
    chief witch on stage 119
    death before trial 10–11, 40
    pantomime villain 122, 126
    Tibb sucks blood from side 40
    wise-woman 1–2, 43

Demdike Bess 32

Demdike Stare 143, 143

Demdike, Nicholas 32

Device, Alizon 1, 3–4, 5, 6, 14, 16, 28–9, 93,
    143
    lames pedlar 3
    played by Cathryn Harrison 142
    takes grandma to Bull Hole 43–4

Device, Elizabeth 1, 6, 14, 16, 18, 29, 110

Device, James 1, 5, 16, 29, 30, 41
    bus 146
    possible torture by Thomas Covell 12

Device, Jennet 1, 6, 14, 95, 96, 102, 110
    accused of witchcraft by William Nutter's
        wife 100, 109
    brings grandma home from Bull Hole 44

Lancaster Castle (1636) 109, 110
    witch marks 100

Device, John 2

Device, William 95, 109

Devil's Dandy Dogs 41

Diana, Goddess of Witches and Queen of
    Phairie 39

Dibden, Charles 122

Dicconson, Frances 96, 98, 102, 106, 109, 110
    claims to have been set up 103
    magic bridle 95

Dickens, Charles 128

Dinkling Green Farm, Trough of Bowland
    64

Discoverie of Witchcraft, The, used as grimoire
    by wise-folk 78

doll used for healing 32

Drayton, William 122–3

Duckworth, John, of The Laund 41

Duke's Theatre 118

Dungeon Tower 10

dungeons 9, 10, 104, 112, 145

Dutton, Thomas 131

Elizabeth, 'Winter Queen' of Bohemia 104

Elizabeth I, Queen 28

elves see fay

Ephialtes stones 57

Evangelical Alliance 142

fairies see fay

fairy armies 36

Fairy Extravaganza 126

familiar spirits 3, 6, 7, 26, 29, 39, 40–42, 57,
    72, 139–40
    female 41
    join with witch spirits 41–2
    travel with witch spirits 91

Fancie (familiar spirit of Chattox) 40, 41,
43, 77
Farington, William 109
Faugh's quarry 40
wizard of the stonepit 66–7
fay 35–9, *35, 38, 52*
and rowan wood 49–50
as familiar spirits 39
dual nature 38
malignant behaviour 36, 38, 39
similar behaviour to witches 38–9, 40
female familiar spirits 41
Fence 4, 95, 96, 114
Fian, Doctor (John Cunningham) 28
Fielding, Yvette 143
figure flingers 75
fire house *2, 3*
Fleet prison 104–5
Fleury, Cross 9, 10
Fox, George 10
Funafuti-Tuvalu stamps 129

gallows, ceremony of the 16, 18
gallows, location on Lancaster Moor 18–19
Gallows Hill 18–19
Gardner, Gerald 136–8, *137*
Garnett, Jeremiah 78
Garnett, Reverend Richard 78–9
Gateshead 22
Gawthorpe Hall 4, 96, *101*
George (stone head at Whalley) 64–6, *65*
George III, King 124
Ghana 137
ghost of witch 144
Gisburn 5
Globe theatre 117
Golden Lion, Lancaster 18
Goldshaw 40

Good Omens 142
Gospelles of Dystaves 34
Gray, Alice 5
Great Mitton Hall 71, 72
Green Bank Farm 96
Greenhead 2
Grimaldi, Giuseppe 122
Grimaldi, Joseph (Joey) 122

hagstones 57–8, *58*
Halsall, Sir Cuthbert (Sheriff of Lancashire)
13
Halseworths (wise-man) 75
hanging, execution by 18–21, *20*
hanging day 19
Hargreaves, Jennet 95, 102, 103, 104, 106,
109, 110
*Harlequin and Tim Bobbin or: The Lancashire
Witches* 126
*Harlequin, Dicky Sam and the Liverpool Liver
or Oliver Cromwell, Prince
Rupert, the Lancashire Witches and their Fairy
Army of Mannikins* 126
Harlequin's Frolic 122
Harvey, William 106–7
Haymarket theatre 122
hearts
as apotropaic design 50
pierced with pins 33, *33,* 50
Heaton, Mrs 81
Henry VI, King 36
Hesketh, Joe 144
Hewitt, Katherine (Mouldheels) 5, 16
Higgin, Alice 102
bone found on person 98, 100
dies in prison 102–3
Hilton, Mary 21
Hipping Stones (Brungerley) 36–7

Hoarstones 113–16, *115*
  boundaries (natural world) 56, 113
  boundaries (with supernatural world)
    114
  haunted spot, reputation as 96, 115
  iron cross found in wall 115
  prehistoric stone circle/tomb, possible site
    of 114
  witch assembly (1633) *94*, 95–6, 97,
    108
  witch feast acted on London stage 117
Hofstadir *42*, 42–3
Holden, Sue 71
Holgate, Christopher 5, 8, 11
at Hoarstones 95
Hope, Thomas (wise-man) 77
Hopkins, Matthew 127
Hore Stone, Enstone *114*
horseshoes, used to repel witches 34–5, *35*,
    42, 45, 46
Horsham, West Sussex 23
Huntroyde 96

iron (used to repel witches and fairies) 35, 39,
    47, 53
iron cross (found at Hoarstones) 115

James I, King 5, 7, *7*, 16, 28, 81
see also *Daemonologie*
James the Glover of Windle (wise-man) 75
Jenny Greenteeth 36
Johnson, Margaret 102, 103
  describes nature of familiar spirits 91
  disappears from records 110
  'penitent witch' from Marsden 100
  witch marks 99, 100, 106
Judges' Lodgings, Lancaster Castle 13, 103

Kildwick 96
Kildwick church 96–7
Kirk, Robert 39

Lancashire Witch (Class 86 locomotive) 130
Lancashire Witch (clipper ship) 131
Lancashire Witch (slaver ship) 130–1
Lancashire Witch, A (painting by William
    Bradley) *128*, 129
Lancashire Witch, The (locomotive) 129
Lancashire Witch Polka 127
Lancashire witches
  ale 146
  beautiful Lancashire ladies, term for
    122–4, 128–9
  buses 146
  comic opera 118–19, 121, 127
  equestrian spectacle 126–7
  fact and fiction, confusion between 141
  locomotives 129–30
  Most Haunted team, fail to throttle 143
  pageants, historical 133, *134*, *135*, 136
  paintings *14*, *128*, 129, 133, 144
  playbill, earliest English 118, *123*
  poetry 144
  pointed hats 122
  postage stamps 129, *129*
  public houses 146
  puppet show at Bartholemew Fair 118, *123*
  Restoration theatre, essential ingredient
    of 119
  ships 130–2
  stereotypical image 122, *127*
  television 142, 143
  toasted at official dinners 124, 128
Lancashire witches (1634) 95–113
  overshadowed by 1612 witches 108, 125–6
  still in prison (1636) 110

summoned to London 102

The Witches of Lancashire play 117–18

Lancashire Witches, The (novel by Harrison Ainsworth) 32, 125–6

Lancashire Witches, The (ballad)
  17th century 118
  19th century 127

Lancashire Witches, The, and Teague O Divelly the Irish Priest: A Comedy 118–121, *119*

Lancashire Witches, The, and the Distresses of Harlequin 122

Lancashire Witches' Gallop for the Pianoforte, The 127

Lancashire Witches, The, or, Harlequin Every Where 120, 122

Lancashire Witches, The, or King James' Frolic 127

Lancashire Witches Schottische, The 127

Lancaster 6, *8*, 8–9, 11, 17, *18*, 18–19, 97, 144

Lancaster Castle 5, 6, 9, 10, 13, 22, 54, 103, 109–112, 144, *145*

Lancaster Moor 8

Lancaster pageant (1913) 133, *134*

Lancaster workhouse 19

Late Lancashire Witches, The, see Witches of Lancashire, The

Law, Abraham 3
  played by James Laurenson 142

Law, John 3, 14–16

Leech Book of Bald 56

Legend of the Witches (Alex Sanders film) 139

Leigh, Mr, of Standish 18, 20

Lilliputian pantomime 122

Lilly, William 78

'Little Ease' dungeon 12

Liverpool 128

Lloynd, Jennet 96, 102, 109
  dies in prison 103

lewd antics on pile of lime 100

Logan, Kevin 142–3

Lord, Janet 86

Lucifer over Lancashire (documentary) 143

maleficia 3, 31, 33–4, 42, 45, 121
  examples of 27, 33, 43–4, 56, 131
  original meaning 26
  protection from 34, 50, 53, 56, 68, 78, 89, 90, 93
  see also clay pictures

Malkin Tower 1
  grand assembly of witches 5–8, 16
  possible remains at Bull Hole 42

Manchester Museum 61, 62

Marsden 100

Marylebone Theatre 126

Melbourne 132

Merrifield, Ralph 54, 60–1, 62–3
  and Gerald Gardner 137
  and Red Pump witchstone 70, 71

Mist over Pendle 141–2

Moor Game Hall Farm, Dutton 63

Moor Lane, Lancaster 8, 18, 19

Moorhouse *infra* Butterworth 86

Morrison, Blake 144

Moss End 5, 83

Most Haunted Live 143

Mr Punch 118

Murray, Margaret 136

Museum of Leathercraft, Northampton 53

Museum of London 60

Museum of Witchcraft, Boscastle *31*, 32, 146

Ned o' Roughs *see* Robinson, Edmund

Neill, Robert
  and Lois Bourne 138
  guest of honour at Towneley Hall 142

Newcastle-upon-Tyne 22, 129

Newchurch-in-Pendle 1, 40, 42, 66, 144
    see also St Mary's Church

Newes from Scotland 7, 7

News from Hyde Park 118

Niazali 21

Norden 84

North Berwick witches 7, 28

Nowell, Roger 3–4, 5, 6–7, 13, 14, 28, 40,
    44, 76
    played by John Stratton 142

Nutter, Alice (Lancashire witch) 5, 16
    refuses to speak at gallows 19–20
    social status 16
    traditional grave at Newchurch 146, 147

Nutter, Alice (singer and playwright) 144

Nutter, Christopher, Marie and Robert 28

Nutter, Isabell 99, 100

Nutter, John 43–4

Old Dorothy 136

Old Hall, Lancaster 10

Old Langsettle (wise-man of Colne) 77–8

Owd Rollison (wise-man of Roe Green) 78

Packer Meadow 86

Padiham 17, 101
    Constable of 4

Painter Wood, Billington 64

Paracelsian charm 82–5, 83

Paracelsus 85

Paslew, John (last Abbot of Whalley) 32

Pearson, Margaret 17
    accused of hagriding animals 57, 59

pebbles, white 56

Peel, Edgar 146

Peg o' Nell 36–7, 37

Peg Powler 36

Pelham, Sir William 97

Pendle Forest, reputation for witchcraft 25

Pendle Hall Farm 2

Pendle Hell 143

Pendle Hill 1, 142, 144

Pendle Witch (locomotive) 130, 130

Pendle Witch Camp 146

Perkins, William 76

phosphorus, discovery of 90

Piazza Euclid, Rome 27

pillory 17, 17

piss prophets 75

Poly-Olbion 124

Potts, Thomas 6, 11, 12, 13, 16, 19, 28, 30, 31,
    124, 125

Power, The (play by Alice Nutter) 144

Pratchett, Terry 142

Preston, Jennet 5, 6

Prestonpans 28, 33

Prickshaw witch (George Clegg) 77

Priory Church of St Mary 22, 23, 23

Prophane Pastime or the Witches Mad Humors
    118

Puck's Well, near Bull Hole, 46, 47

Quernmore Road, Lancaster 19

Read Hall 3, 4, 4

Red Pump Inn, Bashall Eaves 68–70, 70

Redfearn, Anne 2, 4, 5, 16
    most skilled at making clay pictures 28

Rego, Paula 144

Ribble, River 36

Ribchester Museum 54

Rigby, Isabella 22

Robey, Isabel 17, 75

Robinson, Edmund 95–97, 112–13
    confesses to lying 108–9

with father in London 102, 108

Robinson, John 5, 29

Rochdale 77, 80, 84

    witchcraft cases 85–6

    see also Touchstones, Rochdale

Roe Green wise-man 78

Rolls Royce's 'jet propelled witches' *135*, 136

Roman witch 28

Rome 27–8

Rough Lee 5, 144

rowan 49–50

    hated by fairies and witches 49, 50

    holy tree sacred to Thor 49

Royal Circus theatre 122

Royal Lyceum theatre 126

Sabbat 144

Sabden Fold 56, 83

Salem Witchcraft Museum 147

Salem witches 22

Sanders, Alex

    claims to find athame at Whalley Abbey

        140

    fictional familiar spirit 139–40

    founder of Alexandrian witchcraft 139

satanic, witches regarded as 25, 26

Sawley Abbey 61

Scarborough 50

Scot, Reginald, *The Discoverie of Witchcraft*

    34, 78, 82

Scott, Sir Walter 124

scratching a witch to draw blood 89

semi-opera 118–19

Settle 68

Shadwell, Thomas 118–21

    hostile reaction to play 121

Shaw, Fred Kirk 133

Shawcross, Rebecca 53

Shawe, Mary of Croft (wise-woman/charmer)

    76

Sheare (or Shuttleworth), Mary 99, 109, 112

Ship Tavern, Greenwich 104, *105*

Shire Hall, Lancaster Castle 54

Shuttleworth, Richard 96, 101

sidhe 35

sieve and shears 86, *86*

Simon's Cross, Simonstone 56

Simonstone 56, 87

Society of Friends 10

Southern, Elizabeth *see* Demdike (Mother)

Southern, Pat 146

Spencer, John 100, 102

Spencer, Mary 98, 102, 103, 106, 110

    bucket incident 100, 103

    bucket incident on stage 117

Spicer, Henry 126

spirit, christening the 7

Squinting Lizzie *see* Device, Elizabeth

St Andrew's church, Newcastle-upon-Tyne 22

St Andrew's cross 50

St Edmund Arrowsmith 12

St George and St Patrick or Harlequin, the

    Lancashire Witches and the Leprechauns 126

St Helen's Day 50

St Martin's chapel, Chatburn 61

St Mary-on-the-Hill, Chester 22

St Mary's church, Newchurch-in-Pendle 30,

    67, *69*, 93, 110, 146, *147*

    all-seeing eye of God 67, *69*

    witchbottle found in graveyard 93

St Peter's church, Burnley 112

St Peter's church, Warfield 13

Starkie, John 96, 101

Stephenson, Robert 129

stone heads 58–67, *61*

    ancient example, Caerwent 63

Billingsley, John, and 62, 63
Chatburn example similar to examples at
    Rochdale and Alderley Edge 62
common features 63
Dinkling Green Farm 64
farm animals, protective of 64
George, at Whalley 64–6, 65
Painter Wood, Billington 64
panel head at Lamb Club, Barrowford 66
plaster, protects Beech Grove, Chatburn
    58, 60, 61
protective device, general 58
shooting target, used as 63
walled up in houses 63, 64–6
wizard of the stonepit, Faugh's quarry
    66–7, 67
stone objects 55–56
    see also hagstones; stone heads; witchstones
Stonewell, Lancaster 10
Stratton, John 142

Table of the Sun, The 79
Tannett, Mr and Mrs 120, 122
teeth as toothache remedy 30
Tempest family, Waddow Hall 36
Theatre Royal, Drury Lane 118, 119
Theatre Royal, Liverpool 126
Theatre Royale, Manchester 122, 127
Thor 43, 49
Thules, John 6
thunderstones 56
Tibb,
    companion of Robin Goodfellow 47
    familiar spirit of Demdike 40, 41, 67
Tiburn (Lancaster) see Gallows Hill
Tomkyns, Nathaniel 117
Touchstones, Rochdale 32, 62
Towneley Hall 19, 142, 146

Transdev 146
Trawden 93
Trawden Forest 3
Trial of Witches 14, 133
Trough of Bowland 8, 9, 64
Tyburn jig, dancing the 21
Tyburn Tree (London gallows) 19, 20

urine, uses of 90

Voodoo 32
voodoo dolls see clay pictures

Waddow Hall 36
walled in bride 64
wart well, Simonstone 56
Water Witches 75
Webster, John 105, 108
    body searches for witch marks 74, 101–2
    Edmund Robinson 96–7
    Great Mitton Hall 71
    wise-folk, attitude to 75
Well Tower see Witches' Tower, The
West Bradford, near Clitheroe 78
West Close 2, 95
Whalley 17, 64
Whalley Abbey 32, 61, 64, 139, 140
Wheatley Lane, near Fence 95
Whitehat, Jemmy (wise-man of Heywood) 86
Whittle, Anne see Chattox (Mother)
Whittle, Sir Frank 136
whorls and maze patterns (as hearth
    protection) 52
Wicca 32, 136, 138, 139, 141
Wigan 112
Williamson, Cecil 31, 136
    fails to lend items for witchcraft exhibition
    146

wanted to open witch museum in Pendle 146

Williamson Park 21

Windle, near St Helens 17, 75

wise-folk, services offered by 74

witch bottles 89–93
    Back Lane, Trawden 92, 93
    graveyard, St Mary's church 93
    ingredients 89
    method of use 90–2
    usual find spots 92

witch marks 4, 98–9, 100, 101–2, 107

witch posts 50–1, 52
    Gollinrod, near Summerseat 51
    Higher Constable Lee 51
    human face 51
    location in house 50, 51
    Newchurch-in-Rossendale 51
    rowan wood, made of 50

Witch Wife, The, A Tale of Malkin Tower 126, 127

Witches' Dance, The 118

Witches Galore (shop) 144, *145*

Witches of Lancashire, The (The Late Lancashire Witches) 117–18

Witches of Pendle, The (BBC drama) *141*, 142

Witches' Tower, The (Well Tower) 9, 10

witchstones 68–71
    Beech Grove, Chatburn 68
    Great Mitton Hall 71
    Red Pump Inn, Bashall Eaves 68–70, *70*, 71

Wolfenden, George 54

Worsley 78

Worston 32

Wyresdale Road, Lancaster 19

York 5

Zadkiel 78

Further reading

WICKED ENCHANTMENTS
a history of the Pendle Witches and their magic

'An interesting and imaginative new view of England's most famous witch trial, with an especially strong grounding in folk magic.'

Professor Ronald Hutton, University of Bristol

ISBN 978-1-874181-62-0

Softback

416 pages, illustrated throughout

The Pendle witchcraft case is a compelling human story which provides a dramatic insight into the importance of magic in the lives of our ancestors.

This book offers a detailed account of the extraordinary events that took place in Lancashire in 1612, particularly those surrounding James and Alizon Device, the teenage brother and sister at the centre of the case.

It draws on a wealth of sources, including books of magic and trial records, to evoke a world of magicians and cunning folk, of charms, divination and familiar spirits. It is illustrated with photographs of magical objects in the Museum of Witchcraft in Cornwall, and of a modern family recreating seventeenth-century spells and rituals.

Taking a thought-provoking new approach to the history of witchcraft, it conjures a vivid picture of what it was like to be someone who practised magic during the witch-hunts.

THE WONDERFUL DISCOVERY OF WITCHES IN THE COUNTY OF LANCASTER

Thomas Potts's original account modernised & introduced by ROBERT POOLE

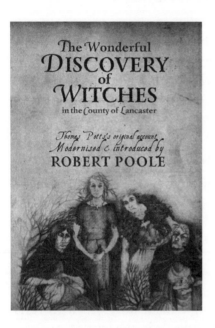

The original and definitive account of one of England's most famous witch trials, now updated

ISBN 978-1-874181-78-1

Softback

192 pages

The Wonderful Discovery of Witches in the County of Lancaster is the original and definitive account of the Pendle witch trials of 1612. No fewer than twenty Lancashire witches were sent for trial in Lancaster, and ten were hanged. Uniquely, the proceedings were written up by clerk of the court Thomas Potts, and in an age before newspapers, it is the only one available: everything we know about the Lancashire witches we know because of Potts.

Historian Robert Poole has sensitively modernised the text, retaining all the information but at last making it accessible for twenty-first century readers. An extended introduction reconstructs the events of 1612, from first accusation to the trial and executions, and traces the remarkable influence of Thomas Potts's book down the ages to the present day.

To buy these and a wide range
of other history books,
visit www.carnegiepublishing.com
or call us on
01524 840111